I0499938

Options Trading for Beginners

The Simplified Crash Course to Create Passive Income. Basic Explained Strategies to Invest in Options Trading.

A Step by Step Trading Plan to Manage your Emotions

By Paul Cohen

© Copyright 2019 - All rights reserved.

The content contained within this book may not be reproduced, duplicated or transmitted without direct written permission from the author or the publisher.

Under no circumstances will any blame or legal responsibility be held against the publisher, or author, for any damages, reparation, or monetary loss due to the information contained within this book. Either directly or indirectly.

Legal Notice:

This book is copyright protected. This book is only for personal use. You cannot amend, distribute, sell, use, quote or paraphrase any part, or the content within this book, without the consent of the author or publisher.

Disclaimer Notice:

Please note the information contained within this document is for educational and entertainment purposes only. All effort has been executed to present accurate, up to date, and reliable, complete information. No warranties of any kind are declared or implied. Readers acknowledge that the author is not engaging in the rendering of legal, financial, medical or professional advice. The content within this book has been derived from various sources. Please consult a licensed professional before attempting any techniques outlined in this book.

By reading this document, the reader agrees that under no circumstances is the author responsible for any losses, direct or indirect, which are incurred as a result of the use of information contained within this document, including, but not limited to, — errors, omissions, or inaccuracies.

Table of Contents

Introduction

Congratulations on purchasing *Options Trading for Beginners* and thank you for doing so.

The following chapters will discuss everything an individual willing to get into Options Trading will need to know and apply in order to become successful and make a reasonable income from the same. This is a form of a crash course for people who want to create a passive income even if they have a day job.

Chapter one is a comprehensive introduction into Options trading basics. The chapter provides an explanation of the different types of Options Trading such as Put Options, Call Options, European-style, and American-style options. The chapters further discuss the advantages of options trading, the terminologies common in this type of business and the pricing fundamental.

Anything to do with trading comes with risks involved, and this is the topic that chapter two will cover. It goes into detail to explain the technical strategies, exits and drawdowns can help a trader to reduce his or her chances of making bad losses. Furthermore, the chapter gives an explanation as to the importance of self-discipline in Options Trading.

The third chapter is about the various options trading platforms and tools a new trader needs to be aware of. The chapter provides a comprehensive outline of some of the best platforms and it later explains how an individual can open an account. Chapter four is about Financial leverage, and it offers an explanation into what it is and the advantages a trader will experience as a result. The chapter also explains some of the disadvantages of financial leverage and finally how to handle the risks.

Chapter five is an in-depth study of the basics of Technical Analysis, its history, and its characteristics. It explains much about support and resistance, the types of charts an options trader will encounter. The chapter continues to explain the secrets in technical analysis an individual should be aware of and the application of the same. Chapter six explains the various trading strategies beginners can use, which include covered calls, collars, call spreads, and put spreads and it emphasizes the importance of practice.

Chapter seven explains how an Options trader should manage his or her emotions, how to handle winning and losing, and the mindset they should always keep. Furthermore, it explains the various mistakes beginners make and the things they need to avoid them. Chapter eight is about the Options Trading market environment, with emphasis on trends and ranges, counter-trends, and turning points.

Chapter nine dives into the key influencers of Options prices which include volatility, time value and decay, interest rates and dividends, and moneyness. The final chapter is about how an individual can experience success in Options trading. It goes into detail on how to succeed on calls and puts and buying and selling calls and puts. The chapter closes with a list of the mistakes every options trader needs to avoid to achieve success.

There are plenty of books on the market on this topic, thank you again for selecting this one! Every effort has been made to guarantee that the data is as helpful as possible, please enjoy!

Chapter 1: Options Basics

Types of Options Trading

There are several different types of options trading and players in this field group them in a number of ways. However, in a wider sense, there are two main types of trading, i.e., puts and calls. Puts give traders the right to sell and calls give them the right to purchase the underlying asset. Options have two classifications; they are either European or American-style options. This has to do with the date of expiry, not the geographical area.

The main types of options trading are:

1. Puts

2. Calls

3. European style

4. American style

Put Options

Traders who are holding put options have the right to sell the underlying security in the future at a fixed price. They purchase these types of options when they think the price of the underlying security or stock is likely to go down in the future. A put option holder is likely to experience one of three outcomes, i.e.:

1. Out of money, which happens when the strike price is lower than the stock price,

2. In the money, which happens when the strike price is higher than the stock price, and

3. At the money, this happens when the strike price and stock price are equal.

With this option type, a trader's outlook of the market is bearish in nature. Traders purchasing put contracts pay a price that gives them the right to go ahead and sell the relevant underlying asset by a predetermined date at a predetermined price. This is what players in this field refer to as exercising an option. Put options are a useful hedging tool and an excellent and flexible instrument for leverage.

Benefits of Trading Put Options

1. They are useful to traders and investors because they can be used in several different ways

2. They can potentially offer a decent return without the higher risk of short selling

3. Investors and traders can hedge against any potential fall in the price of any security they already own

4. Traders and investors can make money from a fall in the value of any particular security without having to trade in margin

5. They allow traders to limit their exposure to risk

6. Investors can limit their losses to the amount they had paid for puts bought based on stock

7. Investors can use puts as a leverage tool to boost potential returns on the capital they invest

The easiest way to trade put options is to open a trading account through an online broker and authorize the broker to execute transactions by simply accessing one's online account. This is also the cheapest way to buy and sell these types of options contracts.

Call Options

These types of options are the most popular among traders. They give investors who own them the right to buy the underlying asset at a fixed price at some point either at the expiration date or before the contract expires. Traders who own call options pay a price to buy the contract but are not obligated to do so. However, if they decide to proceed with purchasing the underlying asset, which is what people call exercising an option, the seller has to sell the asset.

A call option is a contract between the writer or seller and the holder or owner of the call. This financial contract contains the expiration date, information about the underlying security, and the terms of the strike price. For example, if an investor purchased a call based on the shares in ABC Corporation, then he or she would be buying the right to purchase shares in that corporation at a certain price. The holder of a call contract can experience three distinct outcomes, i.e., out of the money, in the money, and at the money.

1. Out of money, which happens when the security price is less than the strike price,

2. In the money, which happens when the security price is higher than the strike price, and

3. At the money, this happens when the security price and strike price are equal.

Investors should purchase a call if they think the price of the underlying asset is likely to rise. On the other hand, if they believe the price is likely to fall, they should sell the calls. Some of the benefits of trading call options include:

1. It is a great way to leverage price movements of different securities without having to own them.

2. Losses are limited to the amount an individual paid for the contract.

3. If the price of the underlying security goes up, investors can either exercise their option to purchase the security or sell the contract at a profit.

4. Call options are great tools for hedging against changes in the price of investments an individual already owns.

European-Style and American-Style Options

All types of options contracts use either a European-style or American-style contract. An individual must exercise the former one on a fixed expiration date, whereas he or she must exercise the latter at any point prior to the expiration date. The cost of purchasing European-style options is usually lower because they are less common. Although the American-style options are generally more expensive than their European counterparts are, they are far more popular.

Sellers of European-style contracts have the advantages of less risk and a fixed timeline since they are not exposed to the likelihood of the contracts being exercised before their expiration date. However, American style contracts have an advantage over European style contracts when it comes to the flexibility they offer. Holders of these contracts have the right to exercise at any time, which gives them options that can help them maximize their returns.

In addition, options trading can be classified based on the underlying asset, their cycle of expiration, and the way in which they are traded. There are several other specific subtypes, such as over the counter options, exchange-traded options, cash-settled options, option type by underlying security, option type by expiration, exotic options, and employee stock options.

Advantages of Options Trading

It is easy to see why this type of trading is appealing to so many people. Options trading offers investors and traders many benefits, one of which is that this investment strategy requires people to commit less capital to an investment than any other type of market trade or stock requires. Nevertheless, investors can still make as much or even more profit as with other types of market trades. Essentially, traders can get more profits for a smaller investment.

It is also relatively easy to learn and do, as opposed to trading other more complicated financial instruments. Options are robust and flexible financial instruments that allow traders to increase their ability to generate profits far beyond traditional short and long strategies. For instance, traders can still earn a profit even when they do not expect any movement in the price of the underlying security. Actually, this is the preferred outcome of a short-premium trade.

In spite of one's unique approach to trading, adding options trading to one's trading arsenal will likely boost one's ability to generate returns in any type of market condition. For example, long-term owners of particular security who expect no movement in the near future can sell a covered call option to generate some profits. Some of the advantages of options trading are:

Market and Portfolio Risk Mitigation

Risk mitigation is one of the most important considerations in a trader's portfolio. For example, investors can protect their underlying security holdings from negative price fluctuations by purchasing a put option. The cost of doing this is the option premium they pay. However, they may have to purchase another put, or alternatively roll their position forward when the option expires. Fortunately, investors can adjust the option premium by purchasing more or less price protection. An out-of-the-money option, for example, is less expensive than an at-the-money option.

Cost Efficiency and Capital Outlay

Investors do not need to come up with a large amount of money to make significant returns, which is one of the main advantages of trading options. As a result, this type of trading is ideal for individuals with a modest capital outlay as well as those with massive budgets. The ability to make huge returns from a smaller investment is mostly due to the use of leverage. Essentially, investors can use leverage to gain more trading power from their capital.

For example, a trader has $2,000 to invest and chooses to purchase Company ABC stock, currently trading at $20. He expects the company's stock to rise in value; therefore, he chooses to purchase 100 shares at a total of $2,000. If the stock price did increase by $5 to $25 per share, for example, he will make a profit of $500.

However, he can choose to purchase call options on the company's stock, giving him the right to buy the stock. If call options with a strike price of $20 were trading at $3 each, he could purchase 1,000 options, which would allow him to purchase 1,000 shares if the stock did increase in value. With the share price increasing to $25, he could exercise his option to buy 1,000 shares and then sell them immediately to make returns of $5,000. After deducting his initial investment of $2,000, he will remain with a profit of $3,000.

This is a simple example, but it shows how traders can generate significant profits from any amount of startup capital they have. This also shows that trading options is potentially more profitable than trading any other type of financial instrument. Traders can save a lot of money when they take a particular position on the underlying asset, which enables them to make more profitable and efficient trades and investments. They can even use several strategies to minimize the cost or risk of taking certain trading positions.

Versatility and Flexibility

One of the most significant benefits of options trading is the versatility and flexibility it offers, which is in contrast to most other forms of passive trades and investments, as well as some active forms of investment where there are limited ways to make returns and few strategies involved. For example, even if a trader is actively trading stocks, he or she will face several limitations. Essentially, he or she can purchase stocks that are either likely to increase in value or short sell stocks that he or she thinks are likely to decrease in value.

Of course, there is a wider range of investment strategies that an individual can apply when taking the hold and buy approach and several different moves that he or she can use to choose which trades to make and when to make them. However, the versatility and flexibility offered by options trading mean that traders will be able to take advantage of many more opportunities for earning money in any prevailing market or trading environment.

In addition, an individual can trade options based on a wide variety of underlying securities. In addition to speculating on price movements of foreign currencies, commodities, and indices, options traders can also speculate on the price fluctuations of stocks. Therefore, there are tons of identifiable opportunities for finding suitable trades to make money. Spreads, in particular, offer massive flexibility in the way people trade.

Whether traders are looking to minimize the actual cost and risk of taking a position or trying to make money from price fluctuations in several directions spreads offer real versatility and traders can use them to hedge existing positions. Traders can also use options spreads to earn money from stagnant markets, which is almost impossible to do when trading stocks.

Looking at the advantages discussed above, it is clear to see why people looking to invest should consider this form of trading. In addition, traders can execute options transactions easily and quickly; therefore, one's investment is not tied-up for an extended period as it usually is in most other forms of financial trading. Options trading prices are also widely available from many different sources, especially from the internet, which makes it easier for investors to monitor price movements, choose the most ideal entry and exit points, and plan future trades.

Terminologies Used in Options Trading

The options trading business comes with its own vernacular. People who want to start trading options need to familiarize themselves with the whole slew of terminologies used in options trading. First, it is important to understand what an option is. Simply put, it is a contract that allows traders to sell or buy a certain amount of underlying security; for example, 200 shares of a particular company's stock, for a predetermined amount of time at a specific price, which is known as a strike price.

The basic fundamentals of this form of trading are quite easy to learn; however, the subject becomes more complex when a trader gets into the more complicated aspects of options trading. It is common for new traders to come across terminologies they do not understand. Therefore, an individual need to use the following glossary of terms and definitions if he or she ever needs a definition for a particular phrase or word used in options trading.

1. **Put Option**

   This type of option gives buyers of a put option the right, but not the obligation, to sell the underlying asset before a specified date at a predetermined price. Likewise, the writer or seller of the option is obligated to buy the asset at the strike price or predetermined price if exercised.

2. **Call option**

   This option gives buyers the right to buy a certain amount of the underlying asset before a specified date at a predetermined price. The seller of a call option, likewise, is obligated to sell the underlying asset, e.g., stock, at the predetermined price if the trade is exercised.

3. Exercise or Strike Price

Exercise or strike price is the price per share of the underlying asset at which the holder or owner can sell or purchase the asset.

4. Exercise

This is the process by which an option owner or holder invokes the terms and conditions of the contract. Essentially, when exercising, put owners will sell the underlying asset, and call holders will purchase the asset under the options contract terms. All in-the-money options contracts at expiration will be exercised automatically. In this case, in-the-money means that they have an intrinsic value of at least one cent.

5. Assignment

An assignment is a receipt of a notice to exercise by an option writer or seller that obligates him or her to buy, in the case of a short put, or sell, in the case of a short call, shares of the underlying asset at the predetermined strike price.

6. Expiration Date

This is the predetermined date when the options contract will expire or become void. The expiration date is the date by which the options trader needs to do something, and it can be days in the future, weeks, several months, or even years in the future.

7. Hedging

Hedging is a trading strategy used by options traders to minimize their investment risk by making a transaction or move that offsets an existing position.

8. Intrinsic Value

Intrinsic value is the profits that a trader can potentially earn if he or she exercises an option at that moment and the underlying asset either sold or bought at the current market price. If the intrinsic value of an option is positive, it is in-the-money. On the other hand, people consider it out-of-the-money if it has a negative value. For example, an ABC September 20 Call would have $2 of intrinsic value if the stock were trading at $22, regardless of its market value at the time.

9. Covered Call

A Covered Call is a call option that a trader sold or written against the current stock position. It is considered to be covered by the underlying security, which will be earned if the trader exercises the call option.

10. Premium

Premium refers to the price of an option and is quoted per share. However, it is typically the entire dollar value of the options contract; for example, the price per share X 1000 shares equals the total premium.

11. Time Value

Time Value is the amount by which the market price of an option exceeds its intrinsic value. From the example above, with the ABC September 20 Call priced at $4 and its stock trading at $22, the intrinsic value is $2 and the remaining $2 is time value. However, if an option has no intrinsic value, which means it is out-of-the-money, it's market price will be its time value.

12. Short and Long

For an option to be short, it means a trader sold it in an opening transaction. A short option position is considered to be negative on the statement. On the other hand, to belong means to have bought an option in an opening transaction; therefore, to hold or own it.

13. Time Decay

Since all options have a date of expiry, they are using assets whose time value falls to nil by expiration. This erosion in time value, which varies with the square root of time, is what traders refer to as time decay. Therefore, there is an increase in the rate of time decay as an option approaches its date of expiration.

14. Cost to Carry

This is the total cost involved in creating and maintaining a stock position and/or an option. These costs include the dividends owed for short positions and interest paid on long stock positions.

15. Equity Option

This is an options contract that gives owners or buyers the right to either sell or purchase shares of a particular underlying asset at any time before the expiration date, at a specific strike price.

These are the most common terminologies used in options trading. In the course of working as an options trader, and an individual will come across many more terms and phrases used in this type of trading. The language used by options traders is a jargon-filled dialect comprised of traditional Wall Street lingo. To become conversant with it, beginners need to learn and understand the meanings of all options trading terms they come across.

Pricing Fundamental

Before venturing into the business of options trading, an individual need to have a good grasp of the pricing fundamental of an option, as well as the factors affecting its value. These include the time value, intrinsic value, cash dividend paid, current stock price, interest rates, and volatility. Several pricing models for options use these factors to determine its fair market value. Just like in any other type of investment, traders need to understand what affects the value of their options investment to use them effectively.

The fluctuations in the price of the underlying asset have a direct effect on the price of an option. In most situations, an increase in the price of a stock will lead to a rise in the price of a call option, and a fall in the price of a put option. However, if the price of the stock falls, the reverse will most likely happen.

Understanding Option Pricing

An options intrinsic value is the value it would have if a trader exercised it at this moment. Essentially, it is the amount by which its exercise price is in-the-money. The equations used to determine the intrinsic value of a put or call option are:

1. The intrinsic value of a put option = put strike price minus the underlying asset's current price

2. The intrinsic value of a call option = underlying asset's current price minus call strike price

The intrinsic value of an option shows the potential financial returns resulting from its immediate exercise. It reflects its minimum value. However, options that are trading out-of-the-money or at-the-money do not have any intrinsic value.

For example, assume ABC Company's stock is selling at $40. The ABC 35 call option would have a $5 intrinsic value, i.e., $40 - $35 = $5, because the holder of the option can exercise it to boy ABC shares at $35, and then sell them in the market for $40, making a profit of $5 per share. However, an ABC 42 call option would have an intrinsic value of zero since this value cannot be negative. This value also works the same way for put options. For instance, an ABC 35 put option would have a zero intrinsic value, i.e., $35 - $40 = -$5, because the value cannot be negative. However, an ABC 42 put option would have a $2 intrinsic value.

Risk-Neutral Probability

When it comes to learning the fundamentals of option pricing, it is important to understand the effects of risk-neutral probabilities, which are often encountered in different pricing models. This probability is a theoretical concept of probable future outcomes adjusted for risk. The two main assumptions behind risk-neutral probability are:

1. The market does not have any no-arbitrage opportunities

2. The expected payoff of an asset discounted at the risk-free rate equals its current value.

Essentially, it is possible that the price of the asset would go up in a risk-neutral environment. However, an individual should not assume that risky assets or stocks will earn the same rate of return as risk-free assets or that all options traders are risk-neutral. This theory measures the probability of selling and purchasing the underlying assets as if there was one probability for all assets in the market.

Determinants of Option Pricing

Several variables determine the value of an option. They include:

1. Variables relating to the underlying security, such as the expected dividends on the asset or security, value of the underlying security, and variance in its value.

2. Variables relating to the life of the option and strike price of the option. Both puts and calls become move valuable when the life of the option is long. Concerning the strike price, the right to purchase at a fixed price

becomes more valuable at a lower price, while the right to sell becomes less valuable.

3. The level of interest rates; for instance, when interest rates go up, the right to purchase at a fixed price in the future becomes move valuable and the right to sell becomes less valuable.

4. Variables relating to early exercise. While a European option can only be exercised at expiration, an American one can be exercised at any time before it expires. An American option is, therefore, more valuable because of the possibility of exercising it early. However, the time premium associated with the time remaining can make early exercise less than optimal. Early exercise is more optimal when the underlying security pays large dividends and when the investor holds both deep-in-the-money puts on the asset and the underlying asset at a period when interest rates are high.

Below is a summary of the main determinants of option pricing.

Factor	Call Value	Put Value
Increase in dividends paid	goes down	goes up
Increase in time to expiration	goes up	goes up
Increase in strike price	goes down	goes up
Increase in stock price	goes up	goes down
Increase in interest rates	goes up	goes down
Increase in variance of the underlying asset	goes up	goes up

Common Pricing Models

Some of the most important and widely used pricing models to research and learn about include:

1. Binominal option pricing model – this is the simplest method and uses the assumption of markets that are perfectly efficient.

2. The Black-Scholes model, which Fischer Black and Myron Scholes developed mainly for pricing European options. It works under several assumptions regarding the economic environment and the distribution of the asset price. Both economists won the Nobel Memorial Prize for their discovery, which used the following main variables to determine options pricing:

   a) Dividend yield

   b) Time until expiration

   c) Strike price

   d) Interest rates

   e) Volatility

   f) Price of the underlying asset

3. Monte-Carlo simulation, which simulates the probable future asset prices and then uses them to determine the discounted possible option earnings.

Options traders who are interested in learning how to take advantage of potential fluctuations in stock prices need to understand the pricing fundamentals of options. Knowing the expected and currency volatility in the price of an option is critical for any trader who wants to take advantage of price movements and succeed in this business.

Chapter 2: Risk Management

One of the essential strategies in the Art of War is the one that states that an individual must win every battle before fighting. Trading is a war that involves fighting for profits and against losses. The initial and overall planning is vital in determining whether he or she will have more profits or damages at the end of the trading process. The same applies when it comes to controlling the risks relating to options trading.

What do we mean by options? It is a contract that gives an investor the right to buy or sell an underlying security or asset at a pre-set price over a particular period. The call option is buying an option that allows a trader to buy a stock at a later date. Buying a put option will enable the trader to sell stock at a later date.

The following are the critical steps to managing the risks that are in options trading:

Technical Strategy

The strategies cannot control profits, but they certainly can try to control losses. The technical strategies here are in terms of options trading strategies and technical indicators of the market. A functional plan allows a trader to study the bigger picture and minute details that in turn, help him or her to make the best final option trading decision. The options trader has to understand the market as well as the goal that he or she wants to achieve. This comprehension is fundamental in managing risks and even more so in options trading, which can be a high-risk business.

There are four possible outlooks or perspectives when it comes to options trading. A view is what a trader expects to happen to the price of an underlying stock or security. Bullish outlook expects the price to rise while a bearish outlook expects the price to fall. A neutral trader expects the price to remain stable or relatively stable, and volatile outlook expects significant price swings. These outlooks determine the type of options trading strategy that a trader uses. The following are six options trading strategies that a trader applies according to their suitability to minimize risk:

1. **Long Call** – A trader can use this options trading strategy when he or she expects the price of a security to rise in the future. A trader uses this when he or she is bullish on the stock and use buying calls to try to make profits. There is an unlimited reward, but time decay can lead to a significant loss in the investment. Time decay is when the market expires at or below the strike price of the option. The trader can incorporate puts in a contract to minimize potential losses.

2. **Short Call** – A trader applies this strategy when he or she expects the underlying security or stock to fall. A bearish investor expects the prices to fall and when this happens, he or she sells the call options. It can be risky in that the call seller can experience unlimited risk and huge losses if the price starts increasing instead of

decreasing as expected. The premium decides the potential reward.

3. **Long Put** – In this strategy, a trader buys a put instead of a call. It is a bearish strategy where a trader limits their risk by purchasing a put option. The put option's buyer has the right to sell stock to at a pre-determined price to the put seller. The amount the trader pays defines the risk here, and the potential reward is unlimited.

4. **Short Put** – An investor applies this strategy when he or she is bullish about a stock. The trader here sells a put by selling the right to sell the stock back to them at a strike price, to someone. The trader, in turn, gains a premium from the put buyer. The seller profits if the cost of the stock increases above the strike price because the buyer does not exercise the put but can experience unlimited loss it decreases below the strike price. The premium determines the reward.

5. **Long Straddle** – It is a neutral option trading strategy where a trader buys a put and a call of one underlying stock at the same time. Another name for it is a straddle strategy. An investor can obtain huge profits regardless of the price movements of the underlying stock by getting long positions in put options as well as call options. This gain is because the date of expiration and

the strike price are the same. A trader uses this when he or she predicts significant volatility in a term that is near, and the necessary moves here have to be substantial. The reward here is unlimited, but the initial premium or amount dictates the risk.

6. **Short Straddle** – An investor applies this strategy when he or she thinks that the underlying stock will go through very little volatility in the near term. The trader sells the call and put on one stock for the same strike price and maturity because he or she thinks that there will be no significant movement in the market. The trader gets a net income since he or she will not exercise a call or put if the stock does not significantly move in either way. The risk here is unlimited, while the premium determines the reward.

Additionally, options traders must understand technical trading to apply suitable strategies in trading from the options above. This trading is where they review charts and make decisions based upon the indicators and patterns in the market. The designs provide shapes on the graph that can inform a trader on where next the price will possibly go. Indexes offer additional information on the chart via mathematically calculating price and volume. They also predict where the price will probably go next. It is necessary to understand the four major types of indicators and their meaning to option traders. They are:

1. **Momentum** – These indicators determine the speed of price movements by comparing prices over some time. It shows the strength of a trend and if a reversal will occur. Relative Strength Index (RSI) is an indicator that determines oversold and overbought conditions by measuring a security's speed and changes in price movement. It achieves this through comparison of recent gains to recent losses during a particular time. Overbought levels are those above 70 while oversold levels are below 30. Short-term trading using RSI is best for options on high-beta, highly liquid stocks.

2. **Trend** – These indicators show the direction in which the market is moving, and they move like a wave between high and low values. Indexes like Open Interest (OI) help option traders to benefit from the short-term price movements and trends. Rising OI shows the existing trend is sustainable through an inflow of new capital while declining open interest signifies a trend that is weakening. It shows the strength of a particular pattern.

3. **Volatility** – These indicators show a range of prices changing over a specified period. High volatility indicates the fast-changing of the cost while lower volatility shows slower changing pace. High volatility also signifies big price moves while low volatility shows small price moves. Option traders use Bollinger bands to measure volatility where the bands contract with volatility decrease and expand as the volatility increases. The movement of the price concerning the Bollinger bands shows the status of security or asset. The closer it moves to the upper Bollinger band, then the more the security may be overbought.

On the other hand, the closer it moves to the lower one, the more the security may be oversold. When the price moves beyond the bands, the options trader can prepare themselves accordingly since it indicates that security or an asset is favorable for a reversal. The trader can lengthen or shorten a call or put strategically.

4. **Volume** – These indicators show how the amount changes over time. It also indicates the strength of a move when there are price changes like the market maintains high volume bullish moves than low volume ones. Put-Call Ratio (PCR) is an indicator where put options to call ratio measures trading volume. Changes that occur in its value signify changes in the sentiment of the overall market. The ratio is above 1 when there is more volume of puts than calls, and it shows bearishness in the market. The balance is below 1 when there are more calls than puts volume, and this indicates bullishness in the market. An options trader acts accordingly with the help of the ratio results.

Exits

Sometimes the best way to reduce or manage risks is to exit a trade. There are three ways of exiting in options trading. First, a trader can choose to do nothing if the options do not have value after expiring out-of-the-money (OTM). In this case, the price of such OTM options is in terms of time value. It means the stock price of a call option is below the strike price while the stock price of put options is above the strike price. A trader exits such trade by doing nothing.

The second way is when an individual trade the underlying security after the options expire while in-the-money (ITM). In this case, the stock price for call options is above the strike price while the stock price for a put option is below the strike price.

The third means of exiting is by selling or buying to close the position before it expires. It means that before an option expires, a trader cashes in his or her place in the market when he or she has a trade that is of profit to him or her. He or she can also cut his or her losses and not wait until the date of expiry to close the position.

Drawdown

A drawdown occurs when there is a drop in a specific investment in the account of a trader. A trader looks at it from the peak high, down a trough low and then back to the new high point. The new high can mean returning to the amount of the original top position or going higher than that. A new high peak also enables him or her to see the trough low since he or she can now compare it with the initial high values. A trader can identify the up and down movement of the investment through drawdown. Due to the pattern it produces, a person can work out the risk that faces an investment before partaking in the options trading.

Drawdown examines risk from two different perspectives, that is, in terms of magnitude or duration. Drawdown magnitude is the amount of value or money that a buyer or seller loses in a certain drawdown period. A trader calculates it terms of percentage by converting the loss that comes from the difference in the high peak in the trader's account to the trough low. For instance, if a trader had 20,000$ in a deposit but loses 2,000$, then he or she has a 10 percent drawdown. Thus, the drawdown magnitude, in this case, is 10 percent.

A drawdown calculates any losses in the account and therefore shows the drawdown percentage in profitable accounts as well. The trader above starts his or her account with 20,000$ and makes profits that increase that amount to 40,000$. However, he or she may suffer some losses that bring down the balance in the deposit to 30,000$. Overall, he or she created a 50 percent profit on the initial capital of 20,000$. However, a trader can still calculate that the trader had a 25 percent drawdown since there was a loss of 10,000$ from the new peak high of 40,000$.

Drawdown duration is the period that a trader needs to bring an account back up to its original peak level. Drawdown is the amount of time it takes to reverse a drawdown magnitude. The trader above had a 50% drawdown in his account, leading to a balance of 30,000$, down from 40,000$ after losing 10,000$. If he or she takes five months to recover the 10,000$ and raise their amount back to 40,000$, then he or she had a five-month drawdown.

Drawdown magnitude and duration help a trader to consider and plan for potential risks associated with options trading. The patterns of drawdown provide valuable information about past and future threats. It enables a trader to minimize possible losses from the options trading like helping them to decide on the best time to exercise a call or put option of a contract.

Session Routines

Routine is a habit that ensures consistency and leads to success. Options traders, like any other professional, must also develop methods that will help them achieve success in the business. A trader must not become a slave to the charts and markets and having a daily routine helps a person to avoid that. A trader can take some steps that incorporate them to ensure he or she has a productive habit.

The first step is waking up and doing a set activity before the start of trading work. It could be exercising or showering and then having a healthy breakfast. Read the news to have updates on current affairs, which influence the market throughout and then check the daily charts and significant exchanges. The next thing is to set the session goal of the day that a person wants. A trader aims to achieve this goal by the time the market closes and then create a new one on the following day. The goal is usually similar in amount and consistency in fulfilling them will lead to overall success. A trader can set this amount by dividing the amount he or she wants to achieve in a year by around 200 days.

Next, a trader can find the trade setups that can help him or her achieve the set goal; in this case, options trade setups. Then take some deep breaths to calm down before starting the day's trading where he or she executes their trading plan. Once a trader achieves their goals, he or she can note down what he or she learned so that he or she can know what to improve on in the future. The trader can then head to the gym to exercise or go for a walk to release the day's stress. After a healthy dinner, get 7 to 8 hours' good night sleep.

A trader must ensure that he or she organizes his or her schedules to flow in an orderly manner for ease of creating a routine. He or she must have the discipline to follow a set routine consistently. A good regime also helps a trader to maintain a sharp brain that will help them to make decisions in the market that minimize risks.

Self-Discipline

It is critical to have self-discipline if a trader wants to achieve any success in options trading. He or she must be consistent, patient, and wise in order to follow his or her session routine and trading methods religiously. He or she must be patient with the markets and avoid chasing them out of hype. A trader must be wise and disciplined enough to not be greedy after gaining profits and instead know to move on at the right time. Overcoming the temptations of laziness and instant success through discipline is the key to minimizing risks and succeeding in options trading.

If a trader understands how all these steps function, he or she can be able to achieve success in options trading. A person can trade while knowing how to minimize risks in option trading by taking the points above into account when setting their goals and choosing their markets.

Chapter 3: Options Trading Platforms and Tools

Introduction

Stock options allow people to trade financial securities more specifically stock or equities, bonds, ETFs (Exchange Traded Funds) or mutual funds without making a purchase upfront. A buyer has the option of waiting to see where the price of a particular financial product will fall before making a decision to buy and sell it at a profit. In options trading, you can either purchase a call or put option.

A call option gives you the option of waiting to buy a stock, especially if the trader expects the price to go up. If the agreed price of a stock was $10 and the price goes up to $12, you buy the stock at $10 and sell it at $12 or hold it. If the price goes down you have no obligation to exercise your option, however, you will have incurred a small premium perceived as a cost for the transaction payable to the seller.

A put option gives the option of buying a stock, especially if the trader anticipated that the stock price would go down. Using the same example if the stock price decreases to $8, you buy the stock at $8 and sell it at $10 thus making a profit. If it goes up, you are only liable for the premium.

Trading Brokers, Platforms and Tools

A person interested in trading options must open an account with a brokerage that offers options. The broker can offer one or several platforms for trading with a wealth of different tools. Each broker or platform has its own pros and cons and it is therefore up to a person to choose which options broker works best of them depending on their expertise, preference, priorities, trading style, and risk appetite.

Some of the best trading brokers, platforms and tools in the market include the following.

1. TD Ameritrade popularly known for their think or swim platform is one of the best brokers for options trading. The broker has won several awards including the Best Overall Online Broker, Best for Day Trading, Best Web Trading Platforms and Best for Beginners. They have many educational videos and content about trading options and their platform has a number of useful tools among them risk management tools. The platform is also popular with professional and expert traders.

2. Interactive Brokers is popular for its low costs. It's trading platform, Trader Workstation has been, for the longest time, the most challenging platform to use; however, they have made continuous efforts to make it simpler so that it can accommodate amateur traders. Their latest tool IBot lets you make inquiries by word of mouth rather than searching through the platform. Their lab also allows potential users to test out their services before making a purchase.

3. As its name suggests, Lightspeed requires traders who are experts and very active. Their platform Livevol X offers expert tools including them, analytical tools not present in other platforms. If you are a beginner at options trading, Lightspeed is not the best broker for you, however, if you are a pro trader the broker has some features you would enjoy.

4. E*TRADE has been in the market as an options trading broker for a long time and caters for both beginners and experts. Some consider this the best overall broker. Its options house platform and Power E*TRADE platform offers a wide variety of tools. One major con is that their commissions are a bit on the upper side.

5. Charles Schwab is another good broker overall. They have a lot of educational material that makes it hard not to succeed in options trading. Their costs are also very competitive. The StreetSmartedge platform has a useful number of tools including those from optionsXpress, which Schwab purchased by back in 2011.

6. TradeStation is one of the best trading brokers made for expert traders. This is thanks to the fact that the broker used to deal with software for trading. TradeStation has an array of tools including the Options Station tool, which is very useful in analysis. Many of these tools are also available for sale to people using other brokers.

7. Ally Invest is another broker with low costs. They require no minimum account balance or fee meaning that you can trade with almost no money as you learn the game. The expert traders, of course, take advantage of this and continue to enjoy a variety of tools.

How to Open an Options Account

Once you have done your research and reviewed a number of brokerage firms, you can select one broker and open an account with them.

Step 1

The brokerage firm will give you two options; you open either a cash account or a margin account. Cash accounts make use of the money in your account to take care of your trading activities and costs. A margin account, on the other hand, allows you to trade with you financial securities as collateral including options you may have already purchased.

Step 2

After deciding on the account, you will need to deposit a minimum amount of money into your account depending on the broker and type of account you have selected. Most cash accounts do not require a deposit. However, margin accounts require you to put a lease $2,000 as per the federal regulations. Beware of fake trading sites that con people money especially at this stage. Also, make sure that the broker uses safe payment methods.

Step 3

Most brokerage firms will assess your experience and capital investment and give you a trading limit before you engage in trading. This is the case to protect traders from the potential risk associated with online trading. Therefore, a trader must obtain this approval before proceeding.

Step 4

Check out the educational and research content provided by the broker and do your best to understand it before you can begin trading. Even though you might be tempted to assume that the educational content is just basic information that you can do without, please go over everything provided and look for more, because knowledge is power.

Chapter 4: Financial Leverage

By definition, Options trading is a speculative stock market trading practice where traders try to profit from any future specific stock price movements. It entails predicting the chances of a particular stock price going up in a set period and staking on its resulting future profit. Its concept is almost akin to gambling, but on unknowable stock price fluctuations within a strict time frame. An option trading is contractual and is bound by stipulations within a fixed period.

We are now going to look at four primary areas of interest concerning options trading, as explained below:

What is Financial Leverage in Options Trading?

When you engage in options trading, you participate in what is called financial leverage. Financial leverage refers to the concept that instead of buying the stock outright and paying the full share price amount, you can put up an initial less capital. In addition, based on the type of your options trade, you can enhance the return on your equity within or after the set time frame. Often, the amount of capital you leverage is lower than the actual share price of the stock. This apparent less capital is what gives options trading its appeal.

Advantages of Financial Leverage in Options Trading

You have rights. There are two types of options, both of which have rights: call option and put option. Call options allow you to buy shares at a given strike cost before the expiry of that contract's duration. On the other hand, put options will enable you to sell a specific amount of your stock at an agreed price any time within the stipulated period of the trade contract.

You will own a given number of shares as stipulated in the options contract. We call it the option contract multiplier (most options have a multiplier of x100) which means you get to own 100 shares of stock per option. Any return on your prospect is factored into this multiplier, giving you an accurate figure on your overall investment return. This multiplier is the number of shares that your option contract can be converted into if you exercised that option. You can use your right to sell your trade contract at any time within the stipulated time frame as long as it is before the expiry date.

Your profit margins are highly magnified when compared to directly buying stocks and selling them at a profit later. In an options trading scenario, you leverage your investment at a given strike price against a future rise in the share price of that same stock price. Now, if the stock price rises as per your speculation, the return on your investment will be much higher than direct stock trading. Your profit margin ratio is much higher, as shown by this example:

Let us assume a current stock price of $20. A broker predicts the stock price to rise to $30 in a month. The trader issues a call option to buy the 20call for $5 strike price, which expires in 1 month.

Given an option contract multiplier of 100, you can see below the marked difference in profit margin between direct stock trade of 100 shares and options trade at the specified strike price.

If the final stock price is $30 in a month:

- Direct stock trade gives you a profit of $1000, which is 50% of the original investment.

- Options trade gives you a profit of $500, which is 100% of the original investment.

If the final stock price is $35 in a month:

- Direct stock trade gives you a profit of $1500, which is 75% of the original investment.

- Options trade gives you a profit of $1000, which is 200% of the original investment.

Your initial cost is low. Buying options are less expensive than buying stock since it depends on the strike price at which you purchased the option. Buying stock depends on the stock price, which is usually markedly higher than the strike price. It, therefore, becomes favorable for you to buy a stake in the stock at a discounted rate.

Your call option value goes up whenever the share price rises above the stipulated initial cost.

Your put option value goes up as the share price falls below the stipulated initial cost.

You have an extra revenue stream. Profits from options trading are a source of income for your business. Given the potential for much higher returns than conventional profit revenues, it gives you the ability to engage in much more ambitious business endeavors.

Financial leverage in options trading allows you to settle debts incurred in the course of business. Your business may have a margin account used to accrue debt and leverage the debt in an options contract in anticipation of receiving markedly higher returns. Once you have taken care of liabilities, options trading gives you room to invest in other business opportunities.

Disadvantages of Financial Leverage in Options Trading

You have obligations when you sell, depending on your options. When you are selling a call option, you are obligated to sell a specified amount of shares for the determined amount whenever any call buyers trigger their contract. As a put option seller, you must buy a given number of stocks for a listed amount whenever any put buyers use their commitment. Your obligations force you into buying and selling at strike prices with much higher loss margins than if you had traded at the final stock prices.

Your get magnified losses. In as much as your returns may have a higher profit margin, the same margin also applies to stock prices which move in the opposite direction to the ones initially speculated. These losses have a significant higher-margin compared to losses incurred in cases of direct stocks trading. You end up with disproportionate losses, which can leave you in financial ruin.

You are exposed to higher risks. Losing on your leverage does not depend on an unfavorable final stock price per se. In case your final stock price remains the same as the initial strike price by the end of the options period, you lose the whole of your initial investment. Using the earlier example, you can see this situation:

Let us assume a current stock price of $20. A broker predicts the stock price to rise to $30 in a month. The trader issues a call option to buy the 20call for $5 strike price, which expires in 1 month.

Given an option contract multiplier of 100, you can see the difference between the direct stock trade returns from 100 shares and the effect on options trade when the stock price remains the same.

If the final stock price is $20 in a month:

- Direct stock trade gives you neither profit nor loss since the original investment remains unchanged.

- Options trade makes you lose your original investment of $500 since the call option becomes worthless at an unchanged final stock price.

It costs more to return to your original capital baseline. In cases where you incur losses, it will paradoxically cost you more to regain your initial investment. Look at the following example:

- If you had $1000 capital and lost 25%, you remain at $7500. Now, to regain your original money, you need to make a profit of $2500 from your existing $7500 (which means a return of 33% on $7500). As you can see, you will need a much higher yield of 33% to cover an initial loss of 25%.

- Your put option loses value if the final share price rises above your specified initial value. In addition, the closer you get to the option's expiration, the less valuable it becomes.

The value of your call option depreciates when the final share price goes below the initial cost amount.

Fear of the unknown. You depend on a chance or probability situation to go your way, and market forces have a nature of unpredictability. When leveraging high-risk accounts such as margin accounts your debt liability increases significantly. You become overleveraged and possibly may lead you into bankruptcy.

You are contract-bound. The contract specifies the conditions and duration relating to the option. Terms become void once the expiration period has lapsed. When the market trend on stock prices is not going your way, you do not have the option of opting out as a means to avoid further loss. You will have to wait it out and incur the full loss at the end of the specified period.

You may become addicted. Any situation in life, which promises the chance of a higher return from little or no input, is prone to be abused. When it comes to money, people's greed knows no bounds. You may end up in a vicious loop of perpetual leveraging to gain higher and higher returns in spite of losses. A loss leads to a tendency to try to recover what was lost. The cycle becomes self-propagating.

Options trading in valued stock is expensive. Stocks with lower strike prices will cost you more because they are valuable to traders. Whenever you engage in financial leveraging within options trading, you will prefer to buy options at a much lower stock price, which has the potential to increase in value.

However, options that involve these highly volatile stocks are valuable and tend to cost you more.

You have a deadline. Every option trade has a specified time frame within which the financial leverage is of value. Beyond the expiration date, your options can no longer trade. There is a limited window for your stock to gain profit.

Risk Management in Options Trading

You should only leverage what you can afford to lose. Risk in options trading is significantly higher than typical stock trading. Therefore, Options trading is discouraged unless you have the financial capacity to cushion against significant losses. For instance, if your business has vast capital reserves or multiple steady revenue streams.

Avoid debt at all costs. You should avoid financing your strike capital using debt. The more overleveraged you become, the more likely you are to end in bankruptcy or collapse your business. Remember, the more debt you accrue, the more difficult it becomes to settle it.

You need to exercise financial responsibility. You have to know that addictive behavior may arise if you are not vigilant. Initial profitable returns have a habit of clouding your judgment from the high risks involved. Always be aware that you are leveraging your money on the chance of an outcome that is not guaranteed. Do not get into a routine because those initial profits encourage habit-formation. Given the high margin that potential losses are magnified into, you may end up losing more than you bargained for leading to your bankruptcy.

You should equip yourself with fundamental skills on options trading. You need to know the stock trading options that are in the market. You have to understand all the potential risks associated with each one and make an informed choice as to which option suits you. In as much as you look forward to accruing the benefits of a given trade, you should appreciate their disadvantages and potential downsides as well.

Seek expert assistance in options trading. Options trading is hard for the individual trader who may not have a grasp on the various market forces, which influence stock prices. You need to seek help from industry experts such as brokers. Stockbrokers and brokerage firms, which specialize in options trading, have a vast array of resources to make informed predictions. Such brokers have the experience to identify the profitability potential of any options and will advise you accordingly. In addition to trading via brokerages, your fiscal responsibility remains intact since it falls on the brokers to minimize risk.

You should be on the lookout for valuable stock options. Although the initial cost of an option contract may be high, the return on its strike price will be high. You are more likely to make a loss or lose your entire investment on cheaper strike price leverage. However, you should make such high-stake investments after careful market research.

Chapter 5: Basics of Technical Analysis

Technical analysis in options trading is a way of using the indicators of market trends to influence your impending decision. Remember, trading in options is reliant on probability, i.e., a guess on the future price movement of your specific traded security. You will want to increase your chances of a correct prediction before making any trade.

For example, if your option makes more money when prices go low, then you will need a bullish market, and vice versa in a bearish market. Increasing stock prices characterize a bullish market, and low stock prices are indicative of a bearish market. In options trading, the market often moves in the opposite direction to the majority's expectations.

Understanding this information allows you to make a much more informed decision on the probability of your intended trade to make a profit. With the proper technical analysis, you stand to be very successful at options trading.

History

Technical analysis has existed for as long as market economies have existed. There are ancient forms of analysis used in the past by the early traders from the Dutch East India Company in the seventeenth century. Other traders who used the olden style of technical analysis were the Asians in the eighteenth century. These ancient traders used currently outdated though efficient forms of technical analysis to inform their trade practices. Examples of such antique analytical tools were in the form of mere charts and pictorial diagrams. The Asians, particularly the Japanese, introduced a type of candlestick chart to analyze their financial information realistically. These early candlestick charts transformed into the now known Heikin Ashi charts. Later, the western capitalist economies started using analytical tools championed by Charles Dow, the co-founder of Dow Jones and company. In his collections of writings on Dow theory, Mr. Dow advocated for the importance of financial analysis for a chance at maximum returns from market trends. Dow Theory formed the early foundations for the current widespread use of technical analysis in capitalist economies. Point and figure charts exclusively represented these initial technical analyses. As technology improved, later on, complex indicators such as trends could be efficiently represented on computers. Specialized analytical software programs are now available to carry out these previously complex tasks.

Support and Resistance

In technical analysis, these terms are used to describe the levels at which the directional trend movement of your stock price is halted or paused and prevented from continuing on the current trend. Support occurs when the downward trend of your stock prices is interrupted and paused or stopped in its tracks. Resistance refers to the same effect on the upward trend of your stock.

Let us start by describing support. In a trading situation where your put option would benefit from a current bearish trend, support arises when this downward trend gets paused. The collective psychology of the market is often the reason behind this halt. When areas of support appear, your stock price may experience either of two scenarios. First, reverse its original trend and turn bullish or push through the support and continue trending downwards. Let us start with the first scenario. You see, when your trading option security trends downward and stock prices fall, more people will tend to buy those shares at those perceived low prices. This increase in demand would suddenly drive up the cost of these shares, and the trend would start to reverse and go up. Hence, your put option starts losing money and becomes worthless. As a result, you panic and sell early to break even and avoid a more substantial loss. The second scenario, you can make significant returns when the price continues on a bearish trend. Those traders who sell early end up falling for the bull trap caused by the characteristics of the support.

Resistance, on the other hand, is a temporary pause on the upward trend of your stock price. This pause is a result of the increase in early sales by traders who may want to cash out and break even while avoiding potentially risky losses. This widespread selling frenzy causes a rise of available options in the market. This increase, in turn, causes an apparent surplus of your option contract and drives down its cost. As a result, the share prices related to your stock option falls and follows a bearish trend on a once climbing trend. Just like the example in the support scenario, this temporary reversal of the upward trend may result in a bear trap, and so it is advisable to keep this possibility in mind.

Once you gain analytical experience, you will appreciate that these temporary pauses in trends are an indicator of your trading stock responses to market forces. You can also analyze the trending lines of support and resistance over long-term trading periods. Furthermore, these trending lines enable you to make predictions over the short term on when to enter or exit a given trade by selling early. It is also essential to realize that bull traps and bear traps commonly arise in the face of these supports and resistance.

Characteristics

Technical analysis makes extensive use of technical indicators. These include MACD, RSI, MFI, and finally, CCI. We use these indicators to determine the relationships between the various market forces that influence stock price, trade volume, and their respective trends. The full acronyms will be in the final section of this article.

Analytical trends are already inclusive of all market forces. There is no need for fundamental systematic strategies such as including assets, dividends, and other external economic inputs.

Technical analysis extensively uses charts for analysis. Software programs running these charted data give an interactive user interface where market progress is easily discernible. Various charts are employed to represent particular technical indicators. In addition, these charts offer a way for the analysts to derive varied factors related to the stock, such as trade volume and share price.

The technical analysis puts a lot of emphasis and preference to market trends and directionality rather than static indicators. These trends are derived from the patterns on the charted graphs and are a representation of the market dynamism. The interpretation of such market trends allows for smart predictions on the future state of the markets. In addition, from the charts, momentum can be derived. There is easy identification of obstructions to particular patterns such as support levels and resistance to upward trends.

Technical analysis allows for the integration of multiple data inputs within the same presentation, such as fluctuations over a while of the share prices and trading volume represented concurrently. This integration enables decision-makers to have a comprehensive read on the market forces and their influences.

Secondary indicators that influence market trends such as bearish or bullish movements and put or call ratios can be derived relatively easily from technical analysis models.

The technical analysis derives on the premise that trends in price and trade volume tend to repeat themselves over time due to the collective nature of market psychology. Traders always respond to economic factors generally in the same way as before hence predictability becomes possible.

Generally, technical analysis is cognizant of the fact that markets always trend in the opposite direction to the majority's expectation. For instance, a bullish trend encourages buying since prices are going up. However, the shock from a sudden increase in buyers will force the prices to reverse direction and start falling suddenly. This sudden fall in prices will trigger even further selling frenzy, which will drive the prices even lower. Therefore, the expected upward trend originally envisioned, ends up completely reversing direction.

Types of Charts

In technical analysis, you need a graphical representation of the stock price fluctuations and volume of trade over regular time intervals. This information is essential for you to make the best decisions possible regarding what kind of deal to engage and when to do so. As a result, we make use of different forms of charts to represent the relevant market information adequately. Most graphical charts have two axes:

horizontal and vertical. These are the types of graphical charts used in technical analysis:

a) Line chart. This chart is self-explanatory. You need to plot the x-axis and y-axis. On your horizontal axis, you then mark off periods over regular intervals. For example, you could have daily, weekly, or even hourly intervals whose units are labeled with dates, weeks, and hours respectively. Remember that your horizontal units have to be in exact intervals. Using regular intervals on the vertical axis as well, indicate your stock price in currency units or volume of trade in numbers. At every range, plot the closing stock volume or price using a dot. The dot should correspond to the appropriate time on the x-axis and units or share cost on the y-axis. Finally, at the end of the overall period under analysis, you can now connect your plotted dots. The resulting graphical representation is thus a line graph.

b) Bar chart. This tool plots multiple indicators such as opening, closing, high and low prices attained during a specific time frame in the trading period. In addition, you can refer to bar charts as OHLC charts, with the acronym representing the various price indicators mentioned. These charts are plotted using a group of vertical lines to show the price fluctuation during a particular time frame. In addition to these vertical lines, you also have short horizontal lines jutting out of the vertical lines. These short horizontals indicate the opening and closing price of the represented time frame. We show the opening price with a left horizontal projection and a right-side projection means the closing price. To show a climbing or falling trend, you are required to color code these bar charts green or red respectively.

c) Candlestick chart. These charts are a better medium for you when the market trend is experiencing a reversal. In analyzing indicators over short time intervals, candlestick charts are especially useful tools to you. These charts resemble candlesticks with a thick body and two shadows: the upper and lower, which are short lines extending above and below the body, respectively. These shadows indicate the highest and lowest prices recorded during that specific period under review. The candlestick bodies are color-coded to differentiate the climbing trend indicator from the falling one easily. You can use green or white for rising and red or black for the falling trends. The top of the body is the higher closing price on the upward trend indicator and the higher opening price on the downward trend indicator. On the other hand, the bottom of the body becomes the lower opening price on the indicator trending upwards while it also represents the lower closing price on the downward indicator. Remember, candlestick charts are better at expressing your trends of interest over brief periods.

d) The point and figure chart is an ancient tool used in technical analysis in the past. We rarely use it nowadays, and you are unlikely to encounter it during your trading activities. Point and figure charts make use of a series of X and O letter characters plotted in columnar forms. These charts do not consider time intervals as a factor. The X columns are indicative of rising share prices while the O columns indicate share prices on a decreasing trend. When looking at a point and figure chart, you elicit only the overall picture of your given trade regardless of its time frame.

e) Renko chart. Plotting bricks represent a Renko chart on the graph. Again, these charts disregard time intervals just as in the point and figure charts. In a Renko chart, the overall trend gets more emphasis than the tiny fluctuations in share prices that are common in the market. These fluctuations are considered noise and a Renko chart's purpose is to minimize or filter out such noise completely. You will have no concept of the time frame of a particular trade but will have the big-picture view on the overall deal. To improve clarity on the different trends, you will need color-coding. Green or white bricks indicate a rising price while red or black bricks are indicative of falling stock prices.

f) Heikin Ashi chart. These charts are similar to candlestick charts but with a more aesthetic presentation. To use these charts, you will have to use the mean price values rather than the exact figures during a given time frame or trading period. Because of averaging the price values indicators, you will get a much more summarized form of candlestick chart if you like. These charts are mainly used in Japan and with traders who are not concerned with the exact opening and closing prices. Your color-coding of the Heikin Ashi charts should be similar to the candlestick charts. Green or white for rising prices and red or black for decreasing rates.

Benefits

You are making informed decisions when trading in options. It shows the market trends: bull and bear markets. A bull is when the share prices are trending upwards, and bear means share prices are falling. Ideally, these movements ought to influence your trading in put and call options. With the help of such analyses, you are usually advised to buy just at the start of bull trends and sell only at the beginning of the downward bear trend. However, you should be wary of falling into bull and bear traps. A bull trap is a false upward trend in the market while bear traps are precisely the opposite.

Easy to understand for new options traders. Clear market trends and indicators are easily visible. These trends show you the momentum in the share price of any securities or stock that are on the market. Momentum signals are used to know when to buy or sell which securities. The charts are clean, precise, and comfortable to internalize at a glance and with minimum effort.

Technical analysis gives you a spot-on reflection of the market's confidence in your security. It allows you to identify profitable securities and stock. Trust in your chosen security is reinforced by rising trade indicators as interpreted from the technical analysis. High market confidence in your stock increases your chances of profitable returns when you decide to exercise a sale or when the expiration period has run down.

Easy to calculate other relevant indicators such as put or call ratios. This ratio is the number of put calls bought relative to the volume of call options bought. A high rate is indicative of bullish market indicators, but paradoxically, we know that put options are profitable only when share prices go down. Being an options trader, you should realize that this high ratio is in anticipation of a potential downward trend. As we mentioned earlier, this paradoxical relationship is due to the market trends behaving in a manner that is opposite to most expectations.

You have a variety of technical indicators. You can compare various technical indicators and have a comprehensive outlook on the market. You get to have extensive knowledge when you have access to the different technical indicators, and as a result, you can make better decisions. There is no monopoly of just one type of technical indicator for all; hence, the chances of misinformation are minimal.

You can personalize your preferences during analysis. You can easily switch between the long term or short-term trends with the relevant alteration on the interval scale. These trend indicators are not rigid in presentation with a one interface fits all characteristic. You are free to make alterations to a presentation style that is suitable for you and matches your taste.

Technical analysis offers you a comprehensive outlook on the market. Since many factors and indicators are incorporated concurrently, you can derive the market psychology, price momentum, trends and predict any possible future hiccups. For instance, you can integrate graphical analysis of both stock prices and trade volume using the appropriate indicators such as MFI during technical analysis.

Automation of technical analysis offers you a one-stop point for the input of relevant data, aggregation of charted information, analysis of trends, and processing of the resulting reports. You, therefore, have the proper tools to make a trade entry or exit. You can make this trade at the same point in a sort of deal as you do analysis.

Secrets of Technical Analysis

Always trade with the trend. You should keep an eye on the stock trend. Once it starts trending upwards, you have an opportunity to buy. Once the upward trend comes to a halt, you should sell. As a new trader, you are advised to beware of the value trap, i.e., a false expectation that a once valuable stock will bounce back after a fall.

Make use of indicators. You can seek the guidance of technical indicators while trading. In addition, it is advisable to use at least two indicator sources with the other one as a confirmation tool. However, avoid referring to multiple indicators to the extent that you develop indicator paralysis where you cannot make a trade due to overwhelming information.

Be calm and composed. During trading, all the data and charts and trending market data may initially seem like an overload of information. Just take your time and get to know how to operate the various indicators and before long you will get the hang of trading. If at first everything seems complicated, do not despair, take your tie, and learn slowly.

You should be aware of something called confirmation bias. What you see is what you get. You may end up misinterpreting the analytical chart. This bias results from your wishful thinking and hoping for predetermined outcome in your mind. Always focus and be in the present.

Have a target profit. Do not enter trading blindly without any set target as to what you are aiming. Trading is a way of raising capital, and so you should have a set profit target. This objective will keep you focused on your goal. Also, be ready to accept possible losses and exercise a stop-loss order where you need to stop for a while, especially after a particularly significant financial downturn.

Responsible trading ethics. Technical analysis is not gambling, and therefore you should not treat it as such. Do not keep doing it just for the sake of it or to win an argument. Stick to your laid down trading plan, otherwise treating it without respect may lead you to spiral into addiction and bankruptcy.

Application of Technical Analysis

Technical analysis should be applicable in a manner that gives you an edge in predicting future price movements. As a trader in options, this prediction should be tailored to achieve maximum returns to you. For successful results, you need to make use of technical indicators derived from proper analysis. Examples of the technical indicators you can use to your advantage include:

a) **The MACD indicator.** This indicator's acronym spells Moving Average Convergence Divergence. MACD gives you the momentum and strength of your stock based on its share price movement. From its acronym, MACD uses your average stock price movements to indicate the extent of either a convergence or divergence between the short and long-term indicators. MACD places more emphasis and weight on the short term or recent changes to render output. That stock's most recent behavior will influence your decision to sell or buy a particular stock. This trend may be its crossovers and divergence from the longer-term intervals, as shown on the MACD analysis tool.

b) **The RSI indicator.** This indicator's acronym spells the Relative Strength Index. This analysis tool is also an indicator of momentum. Based on the recent share price indicators, RSI indicates whether you can consider the market oversold or overbought. Bullish markets give signs suggestive of an overbought market while an oversold market will provide indicators that you can find bearish. We use RSI to determine the share price increments and losses from the initial base level over a specified time interval. It is from such price deviation that you may consider the market as either overbought or oversold.

c) **The CCI indicator.** These indicators acronym spells Commodity Channel Index. This tool gives you the movement trend of your commodity or shares. Just like RSI, your CCI can also be used to determine an overbought or oversold market, but it uses the patterns of the share price rather than momentum. The CCI information is vital to you as a trader as you make decisions on whether to buy or sell options based on the indicated trend.

d) **The MFI indicator.** This indicator's acronym spells Money Flow Index. This technical indicator resembles the Relative Strength Index. The most distinguishing characteristic is that in addition to price momentum, the MFI also accounts for trade volume concurrently. MFI makes use of both price and trade volume for analysis. MFI does not just indicate overbought and oversold markets. This indicator also shows whether the price is approaching its maximum high or low value. You also notice that an immediate reversal in price momentum is absent in overbought and oversold markets when you use MFI as an indicator due to the factored trade volume.

Chapter 6: Strategies for Beginners

People who are new to the field of options trading can use several strategies to maximize their chances of making bank. Whether a trader has a neutral, bear, or bull outlook on the options market, there are ways to take advantage of the power of options to make money. Fortunately, an individual does not need to be a financial or investment genius to succeed.

Options trading novices should understand that options are conditional contracts that allow option holders to sell or buy the underlying asset at a predetermined price. For such a right, the sellers charge buyers a certain premium. Should they choose to let the option expire due to unfavorable market prices, the losses they will incur will be lower than the premium. On the other hand, option writers or sellers assume a higher level of risk than the buyers do, which explains why they charge a premium.

Many beginners venture into the world of options trading without clear and workable strategies. Others consider it as an instrument for speculation. Indeed, options can offer leverage, giving traders the ability to turn a few dollars into hundreds or thousands of dollars, a possibility that is very attractive to new entrants. However, doing this without a good strategy is like playing the lottery because the prize is massive. The chances of winning a lottery are terrible, which is why it is a bad bet.

The potential payoff from options trading is much smaller than winning a lottery and it costs more to trade options than to play a lottery. Therefore, options were not designed as an instrument for speculation. Beginners who want to succeed in this business should consider using them as they were intended, i.e., as risk-minimizing investment tools.

Beginner Points for Options Trading

It is important to understand the fundamental concepts behind options trading and the workings behind it before making the first trade. Some of the things new investors need to understand about options include:

1. An option is a contract or agreement between a buyer and a seller

2. There are two types of options, i.e., puts and calls

3. Exchange-traded option contracts are upheld by the OCC, which is the Options Clearing Corporation. During the corporation's four decades of existence, there has never been a default

4. The options seller accepts specific obligations and grants specific rights in return for charging a premium

5. One options contract represents 100 shares of stock

6. Options sellers may be obligated to honor the condition of the contract if the option expires without value, thereby relieving them of their obligations

Types of Options Trades

New options traders often get confused when entering an order because they do not understand which of the basic trade choices applies. The four types of options trades are:

1. Buy to open

2. Buy to close

3. Sell to open

4. Sell to close

Buy to open refers to an order to purchase a specific option, where a trader is increasing an existing position or initiating a new one. In the same way, a buy to close trade is an order to purchase a specific option. However, the trader is purchasing an option he or she already sold. Sell to open is an order to sell an option a trader does not own, while sell to close is an order to sell an option he or she bought earlier.

Popular Options Trading Strategies for Beginners

Rookies in the field of options trading are often too eager to begin trading. They need to understand that recklessness can lead to huge losses in terms of time, money, and effort. Therefore, before trading, it is important to build a solid foundation by having a good understanding of how options work, how they are valued, and how they can help achieve one's objectives. Some of the most effective trading strategies for beginners include:

Covered Calls

Exercising a call option obligates a trader to sell stock he or she already owns at strike price. Some traders will do this after they have seen good gains on the stock. In most cases, they will sell out-of-the-money, OTM, call options. Therefore, if the price of stock increases, they are willing to sell it and pocket the profit.

Fortunately, new investors can use covered calls to earn money on the stock or underlying asset above and beyond any dividends. In this situation, the aim is for the call option to expire valueless. Some investors use a buy or write strategy, which is the act of purchasing the stock and selling the calls simultaneously; to minimize the cost basis of a stock they have just bought.

Generally, newbies may wish to consider using this strategy about 30 days from the date of expiration to take full advantage of increasing time decay. However, this will depend on prevailing market conditions and the underlying security. They may also consider selling the call option with a premium of at least 2%, i.e., premium divided by stock price; however, it is up to them what premium will make it worthwhile to run this strategy.

On the other hand, if the premium seems too high, new investors should understand there must be a reason for it. They should be careful of a situation where they are getting too much time value. Instead of jumping at the opportunity, they should first scan for any news in the marketplace that might affect the value of the stock because when something seems too good to be true, in most cases, it probably is.

Collars

Purchasing put options gives options traders the right to sell the stock at strike price. Since they have also sold the call option, they will be obligated to sell the stock if the option is exercised. A collar can be described as simultaneously executing a covered call and a protective put. Some investors consider this an exciting trade since the covered call will help them pay for the protective put. By running this strategy, they are able to limit the downside on the stock cheaper than it could cost them to purchase a put only.

However, there is a tradeoff whereby the call option they sell caps the upside, which will lead to it being called away. Therefore, they must be ready to sell it at that price. Investors will use this strategy when they have observed a promising increase in the stock price and they choose to protect their potential profits from a downward shift.

Some traders will attempt to sell the call option with adequate premium to cover the put entirely. Others will use this trading strategy in a single trade, i.e., for every 100 shares they purchase, they will sell one OTM call contract and purchase one OTM put contract, which will instantly limit their downside risk. However, it will also limit their upside.

1. Cash-Secured Put

This trading strategy involves selling the put option, which obligates investors to purchase stock at the strike price if the option is exercised. In this situation, they are basically selling the put option with the aim of purchasing the stock after the option is exercised. Beginners who run this strategy should consider selling the put option slightly OTM hoping that the stock will fall below the strike price and stay there. Consequently, they will end up owning the stock.

The premium they receive from the sale of the put option will lower the cost on the stock they wish to purchase. However, if the stock does not make this bearish move, they will still keep the premium for selling the put option. This situation is quite appealing because it is one of the few instances when investors can make a profit by making the wrong choice.

2. Protective Put

Buying a protective put option gives investors the right to sell stock they hold at strike price. This strategy is helpful when their outlook is bullish and they hope to protect the value of their stock portfolio in the event of a downward shift. Protective puts can also help investors manage their anxiety in times of market volatility and uncertainty.

Investors run this strategy as an alternative to using stop orders, which tend to work even when they do not want them to and fail to work when investors need them to work. For example, if the price of a specific stock is volatile but not really tanking, using a stop order might get an investor out prematurely, which will not be good if the stock recovers. In addition, if an important news event takes place overnight and the stock price drops down significantly, the investor might not be able to get out at the stop price. Instead, he or she will exit at the next available market price, which could turn out to be much lower.

Investors who purchase a protective put have total control over when they exercise their option, as well as the price they are willing to receive for their stock. However, whereas investors can use stop orders free of charge, a protective put has to be bought. Therefore, investors who run this strategy hope for the stock price to go up enough to cover the cost of purchasing the put. Some investors choose to purchase a married put, which is the purchase of stock and a protective put.

Call Spreads

This is a trading strategy used when equal numbers of call options are sold and purchased at the same time. Unlike the call purchasing strategies that have unlimited profit potential, this strategy tends to limit a trader's profit potential. However, it is cheaper to implement and can help investors make a profit from any market environment, i.e., as neutral, bear, and bull market.

The vertical spread is one of the simplest spread strategies to run. It is created when the long and short calls have different strike prices but the same date of expiry. It can be bearish or bullish. The bull call spread, also called the bull vertical call spread, is implemented when a trader believes that the stock price will go up before the call option expires. On the other hand, the bear call spread is also referred to as the bear vertical call spread and is used when the trader thinks the stock price will decline before the expiry of the call option.

A calendar or horizontal call spread is employed when short-term call options are sold, and long-term calls with the same strike price are purchased. Depending on the outlook of the short-term call options, either the bull calendar call spread or neutral calendar call spread can be used. When the short-term outlook of the stock is neutral, the latter can be implemented using ATM call options to build the spread with the aim of profiting from the accelerating time decay of the option.

On the other hand, investors who choose to use the bull calendar call spread have a bullish outlook towards stock in the long-term, which is why they sell the short-term calls with the aim of riding the wave of long-term calls for free or for a discount. OTM call options are used to build this type of call spread.

Finally, a diagonal call spread forms when investors purchase long-term call options and sell short-term call options at a higher strike price. This call spread is somewhat similar to the bull calendar call spread, with the only variance being that its short-term outlook is a bit more bullish.

Put Spreads

This is an option spread strategy that forms when the same number of put options are purchased and sold at the same time. However, while put buying provides investors with virtually unlimited profit potential, put spreads tend to limit the amount of profits investors are able to generate. On the plus side, they are cheaper to use and can be employed by bearish investors to profits from a neutral, bear, and bull market.

A put spread can also be:

1. Vertical put spread, which can be bearish or bullish,

2. A horizontal or calendar put spread, which can either be a bear calendar put spread or neutral calendar put spread, or

3. A diagonal put spread.

Practice Makes Perfect

Options are extremely volatile financial instruments and this is arguably one of the main reasons traders find so much excitement dealing with them. Fortunately, their flexibility and versatility allow new traders to leverage their positions and use different strategies to boost their profits and reduce the chances of losses getting out of hand. However, despite its advantages, this form of business is quite speculative in nature and carries a lot of risk of loss. Like any other type of worthwhile venture, successful options trading requires a certain attitude, personality type, and skill set, as well as tons of practice. By practicing frequently and diligently, novice options traders will be able to gain and develop the following skills and competencies:

1. Ability to foresee and manage risk – This will, of course, develop with time and experience

2. Excellent numerical skills – If you love working with numbers then you will love Options trading

3. Good discipline – It is important to keep your head at all times because not sticking to the rules or the strategies you have chosen will only lead to losses

4. Ability to interpret news events that might impact their profits – Sensitive news will always affect the markets,

so it is important to know how to interpret the news and its possible effects

5. Develop an effective trading strategy – Since experts make use of different strategies out there, it is important to choose the one you feel is best for you and stick to it

6. Good flexibility – You should be ready to make changes in a way that will favor your chances of making money or reducing your losses

7. Active learning skills – If you want to succeed, you have to keep learning new things and trying out new tools and resources made for your business

8. Patience – Most of the people who end up frustrated lack patience, probably because they got into options trading with misguided expectations, which the business might not meet within a week

9. Ability to maintain records – As is the case with all forms of businesses, it is important to keep records for many reasons, especially because these will give anyone a clear picture of where the business has been and where it is going

10. Efficient planning and organizational skills

The bottom line is that experienced options traders get a huge thrill from hunting and watching their trades. Much like watching a football game, it is not always about knowing the final score; rather, it is about watching the plays of the different teams unfold. There is no reason why beginners cannot work towards this goal, because it will only take the time, dedication, a willingness to learn, and all the above. Using the strategies outlined above will definitely boost the chances of any individual towards creating his or her own exciting options games and eventually go smiling all the way to the bank.

Chapter 7: Manage Your Emotions with Trading Psychology

Basics

Most people are very emotional when it comes to money. They either get too excited when they have too much of it or get too upset when they lose it. Since trading involves making money, people are bound to get emotional. Even the most knowledgeable traders who possess excellent marketing analysis can lose money very easily if they get too emotional.

Successful traders are always fully aware of their emotions; they understand them and do not let them get in the way of conducting business. They use their logic rather than their gut feeling to buy and sell in the markets. This is what trading psychology is all about. It involves getting into a certain state of mind that ensures that you are able to manage your emotions, which can easily a cloud, your judgment and prevent you from making sound decisions in trading. Some of the most common emotions that traders experience includes:

1. **Fear**

   Fear in trading is the result of a move that a trader perceives to be of threat to the money he or she has or the money he or she stands to gain from trading. People normally develop fear in trading when they have invested out of their trading plan.

   When a trader gets scared, he or she will either liquidate what he or she is holding and take away his or her cash or refuse to take certain risks. Avoiding risks can make you lose on big gains. It is important for a trader to be aware of such feelings and work out a way of moving past them even though this is easier said than done.

2. Greed

When traders experience big or consecutive wins, they can develop greed. Greed involves wanting to get just a little bit more or exhaust a streak of good luck. Greed is the emotion behind overtrading, trading without cash, trading addictions or trading with borrowed money.

It is dangerous and can lead to very big losses. Traders should also be able to recognize this emotion as it mostly comes up when trade plans are falling apart. A trader already in such a situation should quickly exit their position and go back to using their rationale. They should also refrain from basing their decisions on emotional whims.

3. Anger

Anger is an emotion you should always try to avoid because it arises from too much or too little greed or fear. When a trader misses a win because of fear or loses big money because of greed then he or she is sure to get angry. Continued anger can further cause a trader to be irrational and stray from his or her trading plan, a decision that is sure to send him or her on a path to incurring more losses. This is where a number of people give up on trading because they are too angry to put in more time and effort in a place where they have encountered failure.

4. Excitement

Excitement can be a good emotion to have in trading, and regardless of what happens, it is important to remain happy and joyful. However, it can be an individual's driving force to take on more risks and give him or her the convictions to place your money on certain trades without any fear. Therefore, as is the case with everything else, too much excitement is not good for a trader because it can lead someone to act without thinking clearly. It can easily lead to greed and loss of money.

Winning and Losing

Trading is based on probabilities, which include unexpected events that easily cause big changes in the stock markets and bring either wins or losses. Therefore, how a person handles his or her outcome will determine his or her success in the future.

Handling a Win

Whenever you encounter a win, it is important to stay within your trading plan. Never be tempted to increase your trade size and put all your earnings back into a trade in the hope of making more money. Instead, you should keep in mind that the market can plunge when you least expect it to. Sticking to your initial trading plan is advisable and protects your trading capital.

If you normally trade with 1% of your capital, stick to that and risk only what you can afford to lose, because adding the percentage to make more money can easily lead you to make huge losses. In the event the market suddenly plunges, you need to be in a position where you will only have lost a small amount of money. Sticking to a stop loss also limits your exposure to risk. Continuous learning on trade tactics and a review of the rules once again can prevent you from making irrational decisions.

Handling a Loss

Losses are inevitable in trading whether you are new to trading or an expert who has been trading for years. The interesting thing is that losses are not necessarily a bad thing, because it is common to meet traders who plan to make calculated losses to avoid much bigger ones. The trick in managing losses is to reduce risk exposure, which calls for proper risk management strategies. Setting a stop loss is important, as it is necessary; doing this will set the limit of how much a person is comfortable with losing on a particular day or with a particular trade set up.

Stop losses should be part of the strategy and a trader should only adjust them when it is very necessary. In most cases, a person should stick to his or her strategy and accept their loss by closing the position and getting out, if it gets to that point. An individual should also find out what might have caused the loss and what he or she could possibly do next time to avoid getting into the same situation again.

More importantly, people should not lose their confidence after encountering a loss, instead, it would be in their best interest to take a step back and watch the market for a while. Once they make the decision to begin trading again, they should use a demo account to trade and/or trade small amounts before spending their real money.

Win and Loss Ratio

Traders should put more focus on their win and loss ratio rather than the wins and losses. Here is why: Incurring a 20-pip loss against a stop loss of 100 is a wise move as the loss is only 20% of the risk allowed. A 10-pip loss against a stop loss of 15 is not a good scenario even though 10 is lower than 20 because the risk threshold is greatly reduced. The same case applies for wins; a 60-pip win against a stop loss of 100 is not as great as a 60-pip win against a stop loss of 50. The risk-reward ratio comes about by comparing the win and loss ratio.

Mindset

Since decisions in trading need to be made fast and have great impact monetary wise, there is a need for a trader to be in a certain state of mind while dealing in order to be successful. Winning traders possess certain characteristics in and out of the markets that play a significant role in ensuring success and these include:

1. Self-control

Successful trading requires people to have high levels of self-control. Traders with self-control hardly ever get overly excited about wins neither do they despair when they make losses. They exercise self-control in trading and other aspects of their lives. Those people who are generally disorganized should think of cultivating self-control before they can begin to trade successfully.

2. Self-confidence

As discussed earlier one of the major emotions traders experience is fear, however, for you to be a successful trader, you should try your best to keep self-doubt and hesitation at a minimum otherwise a person may not be able to take any risks in the markets and make any big wins.

3. Self-discipline

Discipline in trading is important. It ensures that people do not immediately jump at every good deal that they come across and risk their capital for low-quality setups. Having discipline also ensures that they stick to their trading plan and properly manage their rewards.

4. Objectivity

Traders should be counter-intuitive meaning that they should not follow what the masses follow. Objective traders are able to make a decision independently as to whether or not to get involved in a trade set up. There are several cases where a multitude of traders have been sucked into what seemed like a good deal only for the market to take a sharp turn and negatively affect all those involved.

5. Flexibility

Flexibility is necessary for trading just as discipline is. Flexibility does not necessarily deter you from sticking to your trading plan. On the contrary, it helps mitigate certain risks by quickly allowing a person to move away from setups that are likely to fail and look for better opportunities.

Avoid Beginners Mistakes

Having looked at some of the emotions that affect traders and how trading psychology or a person's mindset can affect a person's ability to succeed in trading, here are a few mistakes to avoid for you to achieve immense success in trading:

1. Lack of being knowledgeable

Most newbies fail at trading because they do not have the knowledge to compete and understand the market. They depend on luck and whims to win in trading. Trading is a serious profession and requires people to put in hard work to succeed just as any other profession would. This means traders should gather as much information about trading, educate themselves and attend as many seminars as they can on trading.

2. Failure to set a trading plan

They say those who fail to plan, plan to fail. This saying applies very much in trading. Every trader must have a trading plan whenever he or she places money in the markets otherwise what he or she is doing is more of gambling than trading. Such a plan ensures that emotions cannot interfere with trading. A typical trading plan can include the market a trader intends to trade-in as well as the time and risk management strategies. Testing trading plans on demo accounts is one way of ensuring that they work properly.

3. Overtrading

Most people new in trading have a habit of monitoring changes in the market, which is not advisable. Seeing market fluctuations can cause them to make irrational changes to their plan like moving their stop-loss limit. Doing this heightens the risk of failure. Instead, traders should walk away from their machines once they put their money in a trade. Another good practice is to stop trading after three consecutive wins or losses. Successful traders also do not focus on their wins and losses while trading.

4. Lack of money management

Managing money, be it the initial capital or wins is important in trading. Successful traders stick to investing a certain percentage of their money and never go beyond this no matter how good a set up may appear to be. They have strict rules on how much of their money they can afford to lose or play with. These people know that things can turn around for their favor or against them, and if they do not know how to handle their money, they will be out of the business sooner than they thought.

5. Poor risk management

Trading requires you to have a risk appetite but the same should also be manageable. This means establishing a limit on the amount you are okay with risking and sticking to certain potion sizes. Poor risk management strategies will always lead to unnecessary losses that an individual should be able to control by putting in place some simple measures.

6. Getting emotional

Having emotions is normal; however, learning to control them can prove to be beneficial in trading. Having the right trading psychology can help you make critical decisions that will determine your success in trading. Getting emotional, not only in trading, usually leads people to make mistakes they would not have done if they had their emotions in check.

Chapter 8: Market Environment

Options traders understand that they can make money in any market environment, even when the prevailing market is not trading up or down. This is possible due to the versatility and flexibility of options contracts; however, some of the approaches used to make money in any market environment are as complex and risky as they are flexible. Fortunately, options traders can tailor their trading strategies to be aggressive, conservative, or somewhere in between when facing any particular market condition.

Whether an individual is an investor or a trader, his or her main goal is to make a profit. The secondary objective is to make money with a minimum level of risk acceptable. In options trading, prices do not always behave as people expect. This unpredictability could cause traders to incur unexpected losses or leave money on the table.

The modern market environment offers tons of opportunities for options traders. However, some risks come with these opportunities. Essentially, the higher the level of volatility in the market, the greater the risk is. Experienced traders and investors are attracted to the options market as a way to make money from price changes while limiting their risk to a certain dollar amount.

However, they have to do it right. For example, builders who only use a hammer, even if they are skilled at using it, cannot build a house. They need to be able to use a drill, saw, level, square, and other tools needed to do the job properly. In the same way, options traders need to be able to use different strategies to build the trading accounts and profits they desire.

They should be constantly aware of how their trades are sensitive to implied volatility, time, and changes in price and adjust their positions according to the market environment. Although options traders are not market makers, they can still benefit themselves by learning how different factors affect the value of different options.

Trends and Ranges

The choice of trading trends or ranges is one of the most important choices when it comes to options trading. In order to make a smart choice, traders need to assess the price movements to enhance their chances of success greatly. Ranges and trends are two distinct price properties requiring somewhat opposing money-management techniques and mindsets. Fortunately, the options market is uniquely suited to accommodate both approaches while offering opportunities for making money.

We can define a trend as a lower high in a downtrend and a higher low in an uptrend. Many options traders spend a significant portion of their time hunting for trends in the stock charts in the hope of riding the next trend to profit. Unfortunately, they forget to look at sideways price action, which can be just as profitable. When a stock stops following a trend and swings up and down between two prices instead, it becomes range-bound.

Range-bound options establish nearly identical lows and highs, thereby creating a lower support level and a higher resistance level. This phenomenon may be frustrating for traders looking to ride a trend. However, the relative predictability of these upper and lower levels can mean easy money for a smart trader, albeit in smaller quantities.

Trend Trading

This is when options traders make trading plays based on stock price trends over a certain timeframe. Essentially, it is a systematic approach to trading based on a stock or assets' current momentum. Traders use technical tools and price movements to identify trading signals. When executed properly, it can be a time-effective and cost-effective way to make money in the options market. However, an individual need to have some stock market and technical analysis skills to use this trading technique effectively.

This style of options trading involves the following:

a) Moving averages

b) Stop-loss provisions

c) Price calculations

d) Take-profit provisions

Trading platforms have a wide range of automated signals and indicators; however, everything comes down to identifying trend indicators and oscillators. That said trend indicators are great since they are the most important tool when it comes to taking advantage of markets that are moving sharply. According to many options traders, trend trading is a sure path to making a profit. Trend indicators help turn the market trend to one's advantage. Some of the most common trend indicators found on most trading platforms are:

a) Bollinger bands

b) Ichimoku cloud

c) The moving average indicator

Trend indicators all come with default interpretations. Even if a trader does not know how to use one of these indicators, a simple Google search will solve the problem. However, applying this interpretation on actual trading can be a bit challenging because trend trading strategies are so diverse. Therefore, the secret to success is to start by defining the market, followed by applying the most ideal trading strategies for that market, and, finally, to watch for any changes that might indicate the trend is about to end.

Benefits of Trend Trading

a) Ability to make a few trades while still making money.

b) It does not require a lot of time, which is ideal for busy people looking to make extra money.

c) It does not require the same daily grind that most day traders have to go through.

d) It is less risky and allows traders to focus on trends within different industries and stocks.

Disadvantages

a) It is not for people who want to make quick money.

b) There is a potential for setting poor guidelines and restrictions because not all trends proceed as expected.

Range Trading

The truth about options trading is that markets often move sideways. It is in such market conditions that options traders do the most harm to themselves, especially when they continue to follow a trend when the market starts going sideways. However, not all range-bound market conditions are the same. A few are simply not worth trading; therefore, it is important to understand what type of range-bound markets one should choose to trade. When the market inevitably changes from a trending condition to a sideways-moving condition, an individual should do the following:

1. Determine whether the market is worth trading. If it is oscillating between certain levels of resistance and support with a good distance between the two levels, then it is worth trading.

2. If it is choppy or consolidating very tightly, then the market is not worth trading because the distance it is oscillating between will not allow for a good risk-reward ratio.

Determining the strength of resistance and support is critical to interpreting price charts when it comes to range trading. Resistance is the price level at which selling is strong enough to reverse or interrupt an upward trend in price. A near-horizontal or horizontal line connecting a number of tops on a chart represents it. Support, on the other hand, is the level where buying is strong enough to reverse or interrupt a downward trend and is supported by a horizontal line connecting a number of bottoms.

Usually, the strength of these zones depends on the trading volume, height, and length of the level. Essentially, the higher the trading volume in the zone is, the stronger the resistance and support zone. In addition, the length of the area will determine the depth of the zone.

To trade a range-bound asset successfully, a trader needs to first confirm the range. Essentially, the price of the asset needs to have reached at least two similar lows and highs without breaking below or above at any point in between. Once this range is established, he or she should simply sell puts near the resistance level and purchase calls near the support level. Experiences traders, however, may use more complicated trading strategies to play both sides of the coin at the same time.

Since the biggest potential for risk in range trading is being on the losing side of the coin, it is important to look out for any signals that might indicate when this will happen. In many situations, a range is merely a short pause or a period of indecision before the continuation of a trend. Therefore, instead of setting a stop-limit order near the resistance or support levels and simply sit back and wait, a trader should pay close attention to important price indicators.

Counter Trend

Counter-trend trending is an options trading strategy that attempts to profit from an assumption that the current trading trend will reverse. It is usually a medium-term trading strategy where an individual holds positions between several weeks or days. Traders who use this strategy rely on indicators, oscillators, and envelop channels to make their decisions. This trading strategy is useful for risk management, diversification, or pure profit.

Essentially, this strategy takes trading positions opposite to the current trend and can be applied at any time. However, traders mostly use it when they see a strong likelihood of a reversal. Usually, people call this strategy swing trading because traders aim to take advantage of swings in a new or opposite direction. Countertrend strategies are usually complex; therefore, experienced traders are the ones who mostly use them.

The idea behind this strategy is to take advantage of overpriced options in the market that is in a decline or incline. For example, if a particular stock is overpriced and has been rallying for a long period; many people assume it will continue to do so forever. Some smart options traders look for such trends and try to take advantage of the possibility of that stock being overpriced because it is in high demand. Ideally, the strategy can make money if the stock goes down, up, or sideways. However, if it continues to rise too fast too far, there is a lot of room for error.

Participation

Many options traders do not understand the participants on the other end of their trades or transactions. Trading in options is mot some mysterious process simply because it is a different form of security. In fact, it is quite similar to trading stocks. In the options market, individual traders are dealing with the following participants:

1. Retail investors just like them

2. Market makers

3. Broker-dealers

4. Institutional traders

5. Exchanges

However, all these participants are generally referred to as traders. Transactions made by each participant are routed to exchanges. Retail investors purchase and sell options using their own money to make a profit. Market makers, on the other hand, are the huge players in the game. They make offers and bids on the options on specific securities and provide liquidity in the marketplace. Essentially, they are usually ready to take a stand on the opposite side of the trade if and when the other participants in the marketplace wish to purchase or sell an option.

Broker-dealers work to make trades happen. These firms accept orders or bids on behalf of their clients and then make sure they execute them at the best price available in the open market. They do this through exchanges for a commission on each trade. In addition, dealers may also choose to sell or purchase options for their own profit, but brokers do not do this.

Institutional traders are large professional trading entities like hedge funds and mutual funds. They often trade options as pure speculation or to hedge their positions. Finally, exchanges exist to provide timely price information and to ensure an orderly and fair marketplace. They can be either an electronic platform or a physical location where traders meet to transact.

Turning Points

These are the obvious lows and highs where markets g from bearish to bullish, or vice versa. Essentially, a market turning point is the area of price reversal. Options trading market turning points stand out clearly on price charts, making them easy to identify. They can create the illusion that profitable trades are easy to catch. However, trying to do so is what causes most inexperienced options traders to suffer losses.

Tips for Trading Turning Points

1. Avoid trading initial market turning points.

2. Wait for another reversal into such a level and try to spot the fake breakout pattern or squeeze.

3. Avoid picking bottoms or tops during such a squeeze.

Options traders should think smart and avoid following the crowd trading tip that leads the majority of traders to do the same, costly mistake.

It is important to understand how to use options to accomplish one's financial objectives because these financial instruments trade differently than stocks. For the experienced options trader, this is a good thing because he or she can design strategies to profit from a wide range of market conditions with minimum risk.

Chapter 9: Key Influencers on Options Prices

It is not possible to price an option unless an individual understands what constitutes its value. This is because a single option trade can morph into a complex process of adjustments, multiple orders, and several strategies. In the broader sense, options prices are made up of two key components, i.e., time value and intrinsic value.

Time value is any amount that is in excess of the intrinsic value of the option. The intrinsic value, on the other hand, is the difference between the underlying price of an option and its strike price. Therefore, options that have intrinsic value are those that are in-the-money. This can be summarized as follows:

1. The intrinsic value of a call option = underlying price minus strike price

2. The intrinsic value of a put option = strike price minus the underlying value.

Traders can use options for several different strategies, from high risk to conservative, to achieve objectives that go beyond standard directional strategies. Therefore, it is important to learn and understand the key influencers on options prices in different scenarios. Changes in any or all of these influences will affect the value of an option.

Valuation Models

The valuation model used will have an effect on the price of the options. There is a difference between theories of options pricing and options valuation. For example, the Black-Scholes model and similar pricing models attempt to determine the value of an option in a way that makes it consistent with the price of the underlying security or asset. These theories assume a business environment where a riskless, dynamic arbitrage strategy with the option and stock or asset is possible, thereby determining the option value as an aspect of the arbitrage portfolio.

According to this ideal market environment, if the model value differs from the option's value, the option value can be traded against the number of shares of stock to identify a position that is relatively free of risk. Constant rebalancing will help keep the position free of risk until the expiration date of the option. However, applying these models in real-world trading can prove to be quite challenging, especially if an individual is not adequately experienced in the field of options trading.

In trying to apply any of these theoretical valuation models, a trader will come to the conclusion that none of them actually works as expected. The strategy outlined above, which is supposed to be costless and riskless in theory, is actually not in practice. This is because positions cannot be continuously balanced when markets are closed. In addition, failing to rebalance continuously will lead to transaction costs. These theories also depend on stock volatility, which cannot be predicted exactly.

That said, it is important to understand that these theoretical valuation models offer some valuable assumptions about pricing that are important for options traders to understand; therefore, they should not be taken for granted. In fact, Fischer Black, Myron Scholes, and Robert Merton were awarded the Nobel Prize in Economics for their theory, which laid the groundwork for the financial model that has transformed contemporary finance. Indeed, because of their theory, options traders now have the ability to grasp every aspect of options pricing.

Why Care About How Options Are Priced

In the real world, options prices are determined by supply and demand, like the price of anything else. It is important to understand how options are priced to make smarter and more profitable plays and decisions. In order to understand how they are priced; options traders need to take note of the following pricing considerations and assumptions based on common valuation theories:

1. The underlying price of an option is normally distributed

2. There are no restrictions to short-selling

3. All securities are desirable and there are no taxes and transaction costs

4. No arbitrage opportunities are risk-free

5. During the life of the derivative asset, there are no dividends

6. For all maturities, the risk-free rate of interest is the same and constant

7. Prices can trade in a continuous manner

Before pilots are allowed to fly, they need to understand what makes an airplane liftoff. In the same way, newcomers into the options trading business need to understand the concepts behind options pricing before investing their hard-earned money into the venture. It can be boring having to learn all the mathematics behind options pricing, but it is worth all the time, effort, and resources spent. Those who neglect to learn how options are priced are likely to fall for shortcuts, which might prove costly in terms of money, time, and effort spent.

It is incredible how some people will take the effort and time to read through the manual of their new Digital TV, but they do not take the time to learn as much as possible about options trading, even with large amounts of money at stake. If options trading were easy, everybody would be doing it. The secret to success is learning how they work and how they are priced. All successful options traders had to learn the math behind options, including pricing methods and key influences on options prices.

Once prospective options traders learn these things, they can better determine whether this field of business is for them. They need to understand volatility backward and forward, up, and down, and understand factors that make or lose money. Essentially, they need to understand the influencers behind every single option price. This is the best bit of advice for novice traders.

Main Influencers on Options Prices

Underlying Asset Price

This is the first influencer on the price of an option. For each underlying asset, there are several options at varying price increments, also referred to as strike price, which is the predetermined price that will apply if the option is exercised. For example, if a trader owns company XYZ stock at $100 per share, he or she could purchase the 100-put since that is where he or she could sell his or her shares in case the company's stock drops in value and he or she decides to exercise the option.

However, an options trader does not have to hold or own shares in a company to trade options; however, the share's strike price will have a significant impact on the option price. For example, for calls, if company XYZ's current stock price is $100 per share, any option that has a strike price higher than $100 is considered to be in-the-money, which is the opposite for put options.

Out-of-the-money options, on the other hand, have no value at expiration. Therefore, if they have no value at the date of expiration, an individual might wonder why it has a value before expiration. Basically, it is because the price of stock changes and there is a good chance that the out-of-the-money options could become in-the-money if there is still some time remaining before expiration.

Volatility

Another factor that goes into options pricing is volatility, which refers to the magnitude of a security's price fluctuations. Extreme volatility leads to extreme price swings and subsequently more risk for stock owners. Different securities have different levels of volatility; however, this fluctuation in price is not constant. This means that a stock that currently has low volatility might become more volatile in the future.

Fortunately, it is much easier to predict volatility than stock price; therefore, it is important for options traders to place themselves on the profitable side of volatility. However, its effect on an options price is one of the most difficult concepts for novice traders to grasp. To determine its effect, a trader needs to look at past stock price movements over a certain period of time, which is referred to as statistical volatility or historical volatility.

According to most option pricing models, traders need to account for future volatility during the option's lifetime. Of course, they cannot really predict exactly what it will be; therefore, they need to work backward to make an educated guess, since they already know the current price and can analyze other variables such as time left, dividends, and interest rates. These variables form the foundation of implied volatility.

Time Value and Decay

The effect of time on the price of an option is easy to imagine; however, it takes some experience to understand its impact because of the expiration date. For a stock trader, time is a friend because strong companies tend to grow in value over extended periods of time. For the buyer of an option, on the other hand, time is not a friend.

If many days pass with little or no significant change in the price of the underlying security, the option's value will fall. Additionally, the option's value will decline even faster as it approaches the predetermined date of expiration. Conversely, this type of situation is great for an option seller, whose aim is to take advantage of time decay, which happens faster during the final months.

Interest Rates and Dividends

When it comes to determining the price of an option, interest rates can be of value. Basically, the value of a call option will increase as interest rates go up. On the other hand, if the trader chooses a call option, any extra money in his or her kitty should earn some interest, at least theoretically. Of course, in the real world, this does not happen all the time; however, this assumption still makes sense.

When options holders get no dividends even when the stock is trading, the situation is referred to as ex-dividend and the value of the stock reduces due to the amount of dividend payable. However, when the number of dividends increases, then the value of put options goes up while that of call options decreases.

Moneyness Factor

The fundamentals of options trading teach the concept of call-put parity. Basically, for every price of a put option, the corresponding call option will have an implied value. For instance, assuming ABC Company is trading at $40 per share, if the $40 call option earned $2, the put option is expected to generate the same amount because any disparity would be an opportunity for arbitrage, where traders would purchase one option and sell the other for an easy and risk-free profit.

Actually, this concept is meant for European-style options. With American-style options, however, interest rates and dividends need to be taken into account. For example, if the $40 stock had an ex-dividend date that came before the expiration date and the dividend amount was $1.5, the put option would be valued more and the call option less because stock price will reduce by the amount of dividend on the date of expiry. This explains how to put and call premiums with the same expiration date, strike price, and underlying security can be so different.

However, the moneyness factor, which refers to outcomes of at-the-money, in-the-money, and out-of-the-money, has important implications when it comes to the price of an option. The strike price and option premium work together to determine the moneyness factor of an option, which describes the relationship between the market value of a stock and the strike price.

For example, if ABC Company was trading at $40 on 01/09/2018, that would make a $40.10 strike extremely close to at-the-money. However, a $39.10 strike would be out-of-the-money for puts and in-the-money for calls. From this example, an individual would expect the call option to be worth more due to the factor of intrinsic value.

The call-put parity is an important influencer in options pricing because it helps prevent unfair opportunities for arbitrage. If these opportunities were to arise, it would benefit market makers, not individual investors.

It is impossible to achieve long-term success in options trading without having a good understanding of the basic influencers and components of options pricing. When it comes to choosing options to trade, it is important to remember that the time value of an option always decays during its lifetime. In addition, when exercising an option, a trader needs to determine whether it is out-of-the-money or in-the-money. Finally, options traders should remember that market volatility could significantly affect options prices. Essentially, the combination of all these influences is what determines the price of an option.

Chapter 10: Tips for Success in Options Trading

Education is the key to success in any field, and knowledge is power. The best way to ensure success in options trading is to understand all the aspects relating to the trade. This comprehension will help you to know what you are doing and also improve your trading skills in the market. The points below cover all the essential aspects such as terminologies to personal qualities like discipline behavior that an upcoming trader should master to become a successful options trader. Such a trader also looks at the mistakes that he or she should avoid in options trading. They provide useful information to both the options traders who are experts and those who are looking to start options trading.

Succeeding on Calls and Puts

Calls and puts are what enable options trading to take place. Options are assets that a trader can trade while using the value of underlying assets or securities. In an option contract, the buyer has the right or chance to buy (calls) or sell (puts) the underlying security. The buyer gets the right to trade the asset but does not have an obligation to do so. The key to succeeding on calls and puts is to understand the direction of stock concerning what he or she wants. Understanding that together with the following factors will enable a trader to experience success in calls and put, that is, options trading.

Understand Calls and Puts

Two bases of options trading apply in various options strategies, and a trader must understand them to succeed in options trading. They are; call options and put options. In a call options contract, the owner or trader has the right but not obligation to buy a certain amount of an underlying asset in a certain period at a pre-determined price. The exercise or strike price of a call option is the price an option buyer can buy an asset until the date of expiration. A call can also mean a call auction, which refers to the time when buyers put in place the maximum satisfactory price to buy. At the same time, sellers also put in place the minimum acceptable price to sell an asset or security in a trade. Volatility decreases, and liquidity increases when there are matching buyers and sellers in such a call market.

A put option is the opposite of a call option because it sells the underlying security rather than buying it. A put contract gives the owner the right but not obligation to sell a particular amount of an underlying asset in a certain period at a pre-set price. The strike price of a put option is the amount at which an option buyer can sell the security before the date of expiration. An investor who buys a put option thinks that the price of the underlying security will drop below the set strike price before the expiration date. A put option's value decreases when its expiration date nears. It also goes down when the underlying asset's value increases.

Understand Fundamental Analysis

Fundamental analysis looks at the external factors that might influence the price of an asset. It evaluates the inherent value of an asset and analyses the external influences and events that could affect the cost of the asset in the future. This analysis enables a person to study all factors and make a decision on the best asset to invest. He or she also learns which stocks or companies that associates with stocks to avoid. It helps a trader to know whether to buy a call contract or buy a put contract, depending on the results of the analysis.

Understand Technical Analysis

Technical analysis uses patterns in the market to predict future price movements. It uses price charts and statistics from the market to study and predict changes in price in the market. It only considers the patterns on the price chart of an asset or stock. A trader must understand the technical strategies, know which one suits his or her needs the best, and use it to make a profitable market and trading strategy. He or she must understand the technical indicators to be able to read and interpret charts and patters with ease. This way, he or she can be able to quickly think and analyze their situations and work within time limits. Time is valuable since the call and put market have expiration dates.

Understand the Numbers

Options trading always deal with numbers, and traders refer to their options trades in Greek terms. They use numerical terms like Vega, delta, theta, and gamma in the trades. A trader has to understand the numbers and how they function in options trading for him or her to interpret them correctly. An individual must know when a quantity refers to volatility or the trade's break-even.

Buying and Selling Calls and Puts

Unless an individual is a professional options trader, a trader should only be a buyer of contacts to limit the potential risk on what he or she has put up on the contract. An individual who sells options contracts takes a huge risk in trading. He or she gets profits from prices rising or falling.

Develop a Trading Style

A trader should develop a trading style that will suit his or her personality by choosing position trading, swing trading, or day trading. Position trading is one where an individual uses strategy that make the most of rare opportunities that come from volatility and time decay. Swing trading is where a trader bets on movements of price over some days, usually up to 30 days. Day training is where traders make small profits by buying and selling options many times during the day.

Interpret the News

Traders must be able to make solid personal resolutions that are in tune with their realities and not just following the hype in the news headlines. They must choose which information is the most useful, and if not, they must be able to ignore the temptations of investing through news coverage. They must be wise in their interpretation of all the information they receive before deciding on the options trading market.

Be Able to Manage Risks

There is high risk in options trading, and a trader must always consider all factors before and during a trade. He or she should examine their investment amount, pick the appropriate options contract as well as follow a suitable trading strategy to manage the risks. A trader should understand the technical and fundamental policies of options trading to maneuver the options trading markets wisely and safely. He or she should use appropriate trade plans and strategies only after seriously thinking through them.

Be an Active Learner

One should continuously learn from their options trading experiences to improve on their profits as well as expertise to prevent a repeat of losses. The options market is always changing and being an active learner will help a trader to keep up with the changes and be able to take the opportunities that come with those changes. He or she should be flexible enough also to learn to accept a loss and move on to a new market.

Patience and Discipline

A trader in options trading must have the discipline to achieve any form of success. He or she must consistently carry out research, keep records, and follow a productive routine to have a successful options strategy and trading results. A trader must also be patient in situations where they are waiting for an opportunity to present itself instead of chasing after every market movement. He or she must control his or her emotions when taking part in options trading to avoid making risky decisions.

Cash Allocation

A trader has to invest their money wisely when it comes to options trading. A trader should set aside a certain amount, of which only 10 to 20% should in a single contract. Options trading is a precarious business. A trader should always be careful not to lose all their money at once.

In the Money Options and Out of the Money Options

One who buys an In-the-money-option buys a contract that has an inherent value, and the buyer pays for this value at the contract price. A trader who buys an Out-of-the-money-option obtains it at a lower price because the asset price is yet to reach the strike price, which will, in turn, improve the inherent value. He or she must consider the options to use when buying a call or put options contract.

Be Simple

One should make their trading as simple as possible and avoid using sophisticated strategies. A person who is compounded risks losing money from the various pitfalls of different approaches when he or she uses strategies that are clearly too complex.

Time Constraints

Options deal with dates of expiration, so a trader has to know the price moves of an asset before investing to minimize the risk of losses. The price moves should have strong trends and volume that increases to stand a chance at making a profit.

Volatility in Profit

Options are investments of leverage and thus amplify the gains and losses. A trader should prepare to see vast swings of profits, as volatility is a part of options trading. A trader should also be able to interpret these swings via the use of technical indicators.

Liquid Options

Liquidity is critical in options trading as it allows possibilities of profits since buyers and sellers of an asset are always present. If an options contract is not liquid, then a trader has the risk of getting a cheap deal because no one is buying or trading it. He or she should always find out the open interest, which is the availability of a liquid market before purchasing an options contract.

Mistakes to Avoid During Options Trading

There are a few mistakes that a trader should always avoid making in options trading. These mistakes can lead to damaging losses if a trader does not heed to them:

Buyback Short Strategies

Traders have to buy back short plans early to profit when a trade is in their favor. The mistake people is to assume that the deal will continue to go their way, and instead of buying back the short strategies, they sit around and wait. In the end, their greed makes them lose money when the trade flow changes against them.

Legging into Spread Trades

In this, a trader enters the various legs of multi-leg trade at the same time in hopes of making extra money from the additional leg assets. However, the market changes usually lead to losses in the extra legs, and he or she remains with an asset with high risks. He or she should always get into spread as a single trade rather than a multi-leg trade to avoid the unnecessary extra risks.

Illiquid Options

Illiquid options mean that there is no competition for the asset since there are no buyers and sellers. It makes the asset inactive, and the resulting options will be inactive leading to considerable losses in the investment. A trader must always check the liquidity of the market and reviewing the options with open interest. Such preparation helps an investor to protect himself or herself and minimize the risks of the trade.

Chasing Markets

Similar to entering multi-leg trade, impatience and greed can lead to a person investing in numerous deals and markets while chasing after the market movements. They blindly invest because they count on the hype of an asset and end up losing a lot of money in several markets. They say the markets are like shadows, which one will never catch if they chase it. Hence, a trader should stick to a specific market with certain trading strategies and patiently wait for the market to produce an opportunity.

Exit Plan

A trader should always have an exit plan ready before even starting an options trade. The mistake many traders do is beginning to trade without an appropriate exit strategy in place. They end up incurring huge losses due to the time it takes for them to plan and implement an exit. They should consider all the factors and prepare an exit plan according to the various scenarios that can occur in the options trading market.

The points for success and potential failure in options trading provide necessary information that all traders should know. Combining the lessons from the two sections above will enable a trader to achieve sustainable success in the options trading market.

Conclusion

Thank you for making it through to the end of *Options Trading for Beginners*. Let us hope it was informative and able to provide you with all of the tools you need to achieve your goals whatever they may be.

From the book, you have learned a few facts about Options trading. Stock options allow people to trade financial securities more specifically stock or equities, bonds, ETFs (Exchange Traded Funds) or mutual funds without making a purchase upfront. These include Put options, Call Options, European-style options, and American-style Options.

- Put Options contracts pay a price that gives the traders the right to go ahead and sell the relevant underlying asset by a predetermined date at a predetermined price

- A Call option gives investors who own them the right to buy the underlying asset at a fixed price at some point either at the expiration date or before the contract expires

- An individual must exercise the European-style options on a fixed expiration date, whereas he or she must exercise the American-style options at any point prior to the expiration date

- Although the American-style options are generally more expensive than their European counterparts are, they are far more popular

Furthermore, you have read that it is important for traders to have a good grasp of the pricing fundamental of an option, as well as the factors affecting its value. These include the time value, intrinsic value, cash dividend paid, current stock price, interest rates, and volatility. The reason for this is that several pricing models for options use these factors to determine its fair market value.

With regard to the different outlooks that a trader can have, which is what he or she expects to happen to the price of an underlying stock or security, the traders can fall in these outlook categories:

1. A Bullish outlook expects the price to rise

2. A bearish outlook expects the price to fall

3. A neutral trader expects the price to remain stable or relatively stable

4. A volatile outlook expects significant price swings

An individual interested in trading options must open an account with a brokerage that offers options. The broker can offer one or several platforms for trading with a wealth of different tools. Each broker or platform has its own pros and cons and it is up to an individual to choose which options work best to favor them depending on their expertise, preference, priorities, trading style, and risk appetite. New options traders entering an order need to understand the basic trade choices. The four types of options trades are:

1. Buy to open

2. Buy to close

3. Sell to open

4. Sell to close

The main goal of a trader is to make a profit. The secondary objective is to make money with a minimum level of risk acceptable. In options trading, prices do not always behave as people expect. This unpredictability could cause traders to incur unexpected losses or leave money on the table.

The next step is to follow the above advice and get into the Options trading and start making money.

Finally, if you found this book useful in any way, a review on Amazon is always appreciated.

The End

www.ingramcontent.com/pod-product-compliance
Lightning Source LLC
Chambersburg PA
CBHW070345220526
45467CB00001B/255